FOOL OF THE KINGDOM

How to Be an Effective Clown Minister

Philip D. Noble

MERIWETHER PUBLISHING LTD.
Colorado Springs, Colorado

Meriwether Publishing Ltd., Publisher
P.O. Box 7710
Colorado Springs, CO 80933

Editor: Rhonda Wray
Typesetting: Sharon E. Garlock
Cover and book design: Tom Myers
Interior illustrations: Chris Perry

© Copyright MCMXCVI Meriwether Publishing Ltd.
Printed in the United States of America
First Edition

Library of Congress Cataloging-in-Publication Data

Noble, Philip David, 1946-
    Fool of the kingdom : how to be an effective clown minister / by
Philip D. Noble. -- 1st ed.
         p.   c.m.
    Includes bibliographical references (p. 191).
    ISBN 1-56608-023-1 (pbk.)
    1. Clowns--Religious aspects--Christianity. I. Title.
BV4235.C47N62   1996
246'.7--dc20   96-12723
                                         CIP

    1   2   3   4   5   6   7   8   99   98   97   96

With love
to my mother,
who bought me my first magic set,
gave me my first book on string games
and continues to tell me wonderful stories.

Publisher's Note

Contents

PART I-THE CLOWN MINISTRY EXPERIENCE

Foreword

A book sure to enlighten, brighten, and make you chuckle, *Fool of the Kingdom* is chock-full of ideas, instruction, and practical advice. But it's much more than that. It's a reflection of its author, who is an incredible human being. Philip Noble is a loving and lovable person whose personal values and commitment to ministry touch everyone he meets.

Most of us, in our daily lives, work hard to simplify complicated things, but Philip's "Rainbow" delights us by taking simple things and making them complicated. We laugh and we learn.

Fool of the Kingdom captures the essence of clown ministry — the heart of the clown — and delivers it with a uniquely Scottish flavor.

— Janet Litherland, Author
The Clown Ministry Handbook
Everything New and Who's Who in Clown Ministry

A smile is the light
in the window
of your face
that lets others know
your heart
is at home.

Preface

Stories, puppets, fools and other forms of popular entertainment share a long tradition with music, dance, drama, architecture, painting and sculpture as ways of proclaiming Gospel truths. In recent years, there has been a rediscovery of the importance of visual aids in preaching and congregational participation in worship. Properly used, the visual arts provide Christians with great opportunities to communicate and celebrate their faith.

Each generation is duty-bound to seek expressions of faith that are fresh and alive. Worn-out interpretations and stale copies of previous years will not do. Our task as Christians is to share the joy of the Gospel with the world, a world that is forgetting how to celebrate. This JOY makes us strong (Nehemiah 8:10), and no one can take it away from us (John 16:22). It's almost as if the world's quest for pleasure at a higher and higher price is being turned upside-down by God's free gift of celebration. This joy is not superficial, but of the heart. It calls us all to participate. There is even an element of sadness in true celebration. Jean Vanier, founder of the L'Arche communities,[1] remarks:

> A celebration is very different from a spectacle, where actors or musicians play to entertain an audience. It is not a true celebration unless everyone participates. But there is always an element of sadness in celebration. We cannot celebrate without alluding to it because there are people on this earth of ours who are not celebrating, who are despairing, anguished, starving and mourning. This is why all celebrations should end with a silence in which we remember before God those who cannot celebrate.[2]

[1]The L'Arche communities began in France in 1964, through the desire of Jean Vanier to "live the gospel and to follow Jesus more closely." These communities for the developmentally disabled and their helpers have now spread to many other countries, including India, Canada, Belgium, Denmark, The Ivory Coast, the United States, the United Kingdom and Ireland.

[2]Jean Vanier, *Community and Growth* (London: D.L.T., 1979), 235.

The Christian clown makes an important contribution. The clown touches all with whom he comes in contact with laughter and joy or pathos and pain. The clown can never be a neutral figure. The clown demands response by his very being. When the clown has this effect, tears of laughter and sadness often flow. These are not opposites; rather, both signify the beginning of a deep work upon the heart.

Rainbow and Friend

Acknowledgments

Since clowning and storytelling are essentially performance arts largely depending on traditional material, it is often difficult, if not impossible, to trace the origins of any particular story or idea. The situation is further complicated by the fact that "new" material is discovered independently at different times and places.

In the field of origami, for example, Spanish paper folder Adolfo Cerceda produced a peacock from a tiny .8" x .4" rectangle of paper. It involved over twenty-four stages of creation.[1] Akira Yoshizawa, regarded by many as the father of modern Japanese paper-folding, claimed to have invented and published the identical model some time earlier. He was convinced that his design had been copied without permission and was unhappy that no recognition had been given to his work.[2] In my opinion, this particular model, while of some complexity, follows logical and natural lines of development and could easily be a parallel creation.

A similar example of reinvention of an earlier discovery led to the creation of the International Guild of Knot Tyers. In 1978 an article in the *Times* newspaper announced the discovery of a completely new knot, by a retired consultant physician. It became clear that this knot was not new at all. It had even appeared in print before, in a mountaineering book published by Californian Phil D. Smith in 1943. He discovered the knot while working on a San Francisco waterfront. Before that...? The publicity given to the "new" knot raised the profile of knots and knotting and brought people with a common interest in the subject into contact for the first time.[3]

[1] Robert Harbin, *Secrets of Origami*, (London: Oldbourne, 1963), 178-181.

[2] The full correspondence lies with the British Origami Society. I met Akira Yoshizawa briefly on two occasions and discussed this with him. I think he would now be more open to the possibility of parallel discovery than he was previously.

[3] G. Budworth, *Much Ado About Knotting*, (Horndean, England: International Guild of Knot Tyers, 1993). This source contains a fuller version of this story.

I especially acknowledge the help given to me over the years by members of the following organizations: the British Origami Society, the International String Figures Association, the International Guild of Knot Tyers, and Holy Fools (United Kingdom). I have given credits as far as I am able to at least one of the sources when traditional material has been recorded elsewhere.

Every effort has been made to trace sources quoted in this book. I would be glad to make good any inadvertent omissions.

Philip D. Noble

Introduction

Truth and Parable

This is a parable of Parable, who had a twin brother, Truth. Now when they were born, Truth and Parable were alike in every way, and they went everywhere naked. This caused no problems at first, for nobody objected to a little naked Truth, but, as they grew and went their separate ways, Truth continued to go around naked.

People became upset by Truth's nakedness and would not speak to him nor would they allow any of their children to have anything to do with him. And so it was that when Truth was fully grown, he found himself to be spurned and rejected by everyone.

Then one day, who should come down the road but his twin brother, Parable. Now Parable was a sight to behold. He had shoes of the softest leather and clothes of the finest silk. He had a cap with bells and carried a balloon on a stick, and he was happy and content with life.

Parable saw how sad and dejected his twin brother Truth was, and he asked him how he was feeling. Truth told him the truth, for what else could he do?

"I am feeling lonely and useless," he admitted.

Parable thought for a moment and said, "I know what's wrong. You see, people don't like naked truth. Here's what you should do. Take some of my clothes and put on my shoes, and then take hold of my hand."

Truth did all he was asked, and they set off together through the world.

And Truth dressed as Parable became accepted everywhere.

SIGNS OF THE TIMES

DWN WTH VWLS

THOSE WHO JUMP TO THEIR OWN CONCLUSION CANNOT EXPECT A HAPPY LANDING.

Food mountains exist mainly in countries where diet books are best-sellers.

BLACKS CROSS HERE
VERY ↗

This road sign was seen in South Africa during the time of apartheid. Someone had added the VERY and the arrow!

From *The Herald* newspaper, Glasgow, Scotland, April 1993.

Why don8t typewriters have separate keys for apostrophes?

TODAY'S SPECIAL
- - - - - - - - - - - -

SO

IS

EVERY

DAY

ANGER
is only one
letter short of
DANGER.

**BAD
SPELLERS
OF THE
WORLD
UNTIE.**

Part I

The Clown Ministry Experience

CHAPTER 1

Beginnings

In 1957, our family had a surprise visit from Brother Ronald, a Franciscan monk. He was a dramatic figure in his sandals, flowing brown robe, and knotted rope belt. What's more, he could do magic tricks. I still vividly recall how he took a strip of newspaper, tore it into tiny pieces and presented it whole again. In the process, he had "accidentally" dropped a small ball of paper which I pounced upon. Marvel of marvels, this was also untorn.

That one fleeting visit was my first contact with a Christian performing artist. Having received a small magic set as a Christmas present, I boldly gave my first performance at the next Sunday school party. Carrying an old doctor's bag and wearing a collapsible top hat, I produced coins from the air — fairly convincingly, I thought. My first fee was a large chocolate coin wrapped in gold foil. Mastering sleight of hand tricks particularly interested me. By my late teens, I had joined a branch of the Scottish Magic Circle.

Brother Ronald

After high school, I went to college to study math and astronomy, and then went on to train for the Christian ministry. Around this time, I began to feel a vague unease about performing tricks. Magic depends on the unspoken agreement that those who perform the tricks will not reveal their methods to the general public. My desire as a minister of the Gospel was to share openly and fully with others without restriction. I do know several very effective Christian magicians and they do not feel the same tension, but it was a real cause of concern to me. That might have been the end of my involvement in performing arts, but for one thing — an origami book by Robert Harbin.[1] I thus discovered a truly magical medium that could be shared openly with others. It involved no secrets apart from perseverance and practice.

In those days there were few books on the subject, and this led those interested to freely share new ideas, models, and information. As paper-folding increased in popularity, more books appeared all over the world. We were encouraged to develop new ideas. I contributed models to several books in the United Kingdom and Japan and wrote the Foreword for an origami book from Singapore. The British Origami Society, which began twenty-five years ago with thirty members, grew to become an international association of over a thousand members worldwide.

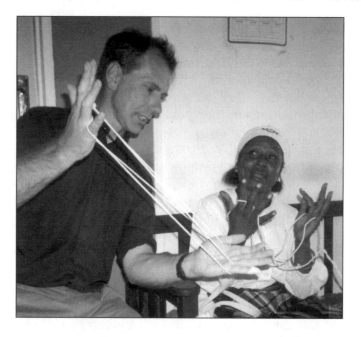

The author learns a string game in Zambia.

[1]Robert Harbin, *Paper Magic* (London: Oldbourne, 1956). Harbin was a famous stage magician and inventor. He discovered origami when looking for a pastime that would occupy his wife during a long hospitalization. While Harbin was not an exceptionally gifted creative paper folder, he had few, if any, equals when it came to promoting origami. His enthusiasm was infectious.

In the early 1970s, while working as an Anglican priest in the interior of Papua, New Guinea, I got caught up in string figures (also known as "cat's cradles"). While many of the natives knew how to make patterns with a loop of string, they were very shy to reveal this at first. It was thought to be childish or primitive by some, and was therefore not to be encouraged. However, as soon as I showed genuine interest and asked for help to make the designs, people happily shared their skills. During three years there, I was able to collect over 150 different designs and the stories associated with them. Though it was extremely difficult to remember how to make even the simplest of designs, I eventually devised a simple way of recording the movements. It involved a series of step-by-step diagrams, similar to those used in origami books, showing how the hands and the string should look before and immediately following each move. This led to my writing a couple of books on the subject and further contacts in the United States and Germany. In due course we formed the String Figures Association, which produces a regular bulletin. All of these things prepared me very well for the next twist in the tale.

Used by permission of Woudi

In 1977, I had the opportunity to spend some time with a clown at a Franciscan guest house in Switzerland. My interest in string figures had led me to an international meeting on children's play, and the special guest performer was a Dutch clown and puppeteer called Woudi. His performance and graceful attitude introduced me to a side of clowning I had never seen before. He used a small stringed instrument, a modern form of lyre, to set the atmosphere and create the right mood for performance. Woudi allowed me to try out his lyre. Because they are hard to obtain, I managed to make a little six-stringed version for myself. This made me aware of the value of simple pentatonic[2] music as an introduction to clown performance.

The people I had contact with introduced me to more and more interesting activities: kites, finger games, trick roping, soap bubble art, storytelling and clown ministry. The latter expression was first used, as far as I can tell, by Floyd Shaffer,[3] and I first learned something about it from another American Christian clown, Conway Barker of the Fisherfolk Community.[4]

I had been showing some string figures to a small religious community with whom we both had contact. They suggested, independently to each of us, that we should get together, which we did. It was a time of rich blessing. Conway was eager to learn more about magic and string games, and he taught me the rudiments of juggling, unicycling and clown makeup.

Then in 1982, the small Christian community that I belonged to at the time gave me a clown costume and wig as a birthday present. The wig was made from lengths of dark red wool knotted through a plastic vegetable bag and held together

---

[2]Pentatonic tunes can be simply composed by playing only the black notes on a piano. This gives a pleasing sound no matter which notes are struck.

[3]A Lutheran pastor, aka "Socataco." He has been clowning around for over three decades now, and he has had a great influence on a whole generation of Christian clowns, including myself.

[4]The Fisherfolk grew out of the Church of the Redeemer in Houston, Texas. In the early seventies, they were known worldwide for their collections of new music and songs for worship. This led them to start a base for their international ministry on the small island of Cumbrae, off the Ayrshire, Scotland coast. Their story is told by M. Harper in *A New Way of Living* (London: Hodder & Stoughton, 1973).

with elastic. I still wear it. It has held up very well. The one-piece costume has been remade and dyed a couple of times. It began with vertical stripes of pink and gray, but is now a deep purple all over.

My clown name, Rainbow, came about quite naturally. I have always loved rainbows. The more I study them, the more amazing they seem to be. Easily seen by everyone, they don't hang around too long, yet they reveal the wonder of natural light and the rich variety of colors hidden within. Also, of course, the rainbow is a sign of God's loving promise for all his creation.[5] One of my favorite stories for clown performances is named "The Rainbow Sins."[6]

Following the first sketch that I performed as Rainbow, I began to receive invitations to perform. These invitations were from such a variety of places that each required slightly different material. Often others, either members of my family or other members of the local church, were involved, but more recently I have had to develop presentations that could be done without the help of others.

Some of the many different places I've been invited to perform at over the years include cathedrals, prisons, schools, shopping centers, churches, kindergartens and outdoor festivals. Recently this has taken me all over the United Kingdom and into Europe and the United States to teach and perform.

Storytelling is becoming a most important part of my performances. This has led me to develop a way of applying clown makeup in front of the audience. I am also working on a new clown character, as yet unnamed, who will be a speaking clown, as I hope to be able to maintain one character through a whole performance.

I have found people all over the world who have been willing to help and advise me. When I've needed information

[5]Gen. 9:15.
[6]This is a version of "The Judgment Day" by storyteller Edward Hays. The original version is to be found in *The Ethiopian Tattoo Shop* (Leavenworth, KS: Forest of Peace Books, 1979). I have renamed it *The Rainbow Sins* and use the version in the appendix with his permission.

about some aspect of clowns and holy foolishness, others either point me to the source or to another person who might be able to help.

Over ten years ago I first heard of Ken Feit, who was a member of the Jesuit order in the Roman Catholic church. He traveled widely as an "itinerant fool," and knowing that he was about to visit the United Kingdom, I wrote to him. I found out later that the letter had not reached him, since he was somewhere in the Sahara desert at that time. Not long after this, I heard he had been tragically killed in a road accident.

Then, just two years ago, a performing artist from France, Sam Yada Cannarozzi, contacted me, as a mutual friend had learned of our common interest in string figures. We have corresponded regularly and have exchanged tapes about clowns, storytelling and the visual arts. Coincidentally, not only had Sam seen Ken Feit perform, but he had been inspired by his approach and had begun his storytelling as a direct result of Ken's encouragement. Sam's performance repertoire includes a series of presentations using string, paper, Indian sign language, poetry and wonderful stories.

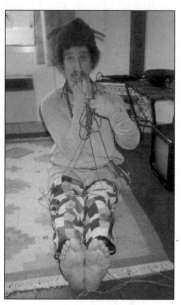

Sam Yada Cannarozzi

Brother Ronald, the Franciscan monk who started me off, has made contact after a gap of thirty-four years. While on a pilgrimage to the spot where the first missionaries landed in Scotland, I heard him before I saw him. Still in his brown habit, he was happily strumming a little banjo-ukulele.

We have shared regularly over recent years, though I have never yet asked him how he did that amazing trick with the torn and restored newspaper. Ronald now lives only six miles away. I learned that he had been a theatre chaplain for some years in the distant past and also performed a quick-change makeup act. One of his characters was, as you might have guessed, a white-faced clown.

Philip Noble and Brother Ronald

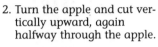

APPLE CUT

1. Cut halfway through the apple from the top vertically downward.

2. Turn the apple and cut vertically upward, again halfway through the apple.

3. & 4. Cut horizontally around the apple, joining the two ends of the vertical cuts. Turn to the other side and repeat this cut.

5. Press the apple hard and give a slight twist. The apple will come apart in two equal halves.

6. The two parts are identical if the stalk is removed.

CHAPTER 2

A Brief History of Clowns (I)

I just fell into Christian clowning, but it has been a most exciting trip. I've discovered various ways of clowning with just a little direct help and training. I've learned many techniques by observation, trial and error, often failing and finding out what *not* to do several times before the wonderful moment of first success. Many of my teachers and helpers have been at the other end of a telephone line or have written with practical suggestions.

This has some great advantages. For instance, juggling three balls did not come easily to me. It took me over thirty hours to teach myself. But the process proved very valuable, as not only did I develop a clown sketch called *The Juggling Lesson* (page 168) out of the experience, but it also gave me an understanding of what can go wrong in throwing and catching objects. Today I am able to teach most people to juggle three balls well in about thirty minutes.

In the same way, my information about the history and origin of clowns comes from an assortment of sources — sometimes from literature, but more often from conversations, stories and personal letters. What follows is therefore not a complete history of clown development, but a series of snapshots and examples of clown-type people.

Every society and grouping seems to need the clown-type figure. He is as old as history. While the role may differ slightly depending on time and place, it is generally a very positive and life-affirming role, but it is never without a certain element of risk. Jesters, truth-tellers,[1] fools and clowns constantly point to

---

[1] A truth-teller is somewhat like a storyteller, but the truth-teller has a commitment to the truth as opposed to simply spinning a yarn, as the storyteller does. A storyteller may simply entertain, while the truth-teller tells his story with a desire to liberate and set free those held captive by lies and false images. The truth-teller is a person of high moral character, while the storyteller may or may not be.

alternative ways of doing and seeing both objects and situations. They are *transformational* characters.

"Turning tragedy into grace is the greatest gift of the fool," writes Peggy Beck, and she goes on to make the following distinction:

> The difference between a clown's life and that of the lonely fool's is that the clown is in demand, necessary, loved. The wave of laughter from the audience, the delight the moment the clown appears is what carries the sacred clown and keeps him dancing. Sadness is leavened when the clown and crowd recognize they are in the same boat, the same ship of fools.[2]

As we look back at the history of fools, we shall see both aspects, and I am grateful to Ken Feit for pointing out a similar distinction in classical literature. Ken, a former Jesuit and student at Ringling's Clown College, became fool-in-residence at several colleges. He subsequently traveled widely, referring to himself as an itinerant fool and storyteller. He noted that Aristotle, in his essay on friendship, alludes to the buffoon and the fool. He points out that the buffoon comes in two forms: he is either the boring, self-important person or the utterly frivolous character. In contrast, the fool is the "grave merry" one, or sacred clown. The latter is the sort of character we will look for in this brief history.

Four thousand years ago, there were clowns in the courts of the emperor of China.[3] One of these clowns was Yutze, a famous folk hero who continually helped the people escape the worst effect of bad leadership decisions. At the completion of the Great Wall of China, the Emperor decided that it should be painted. The construction had already been extremely costly and many lives were lost in building accidents. Understandably, people were horrified at the prospect, yet no one dared to protest. Yutze, who was at that time a kind of court jester, took

[2]Peggy Beck, "In the Company of Laughter," *Parabola: The Magazine of Myth and Tradition* 111 (Fall 1986): 58.

[3]Carol Crowther, *Clowns and Clowning* (London: MacDonald, 1978).

the risk of pointing out to the Emperor, in a funny way, just how wasteful and futile this would be. As a result of his skill and courage, the plan was called off.

Bali has a long tradition of clowns also. The most popular formed a kind of double act, in which one person (Penasor) always worried and fussed and tried to be on his best behavior, while the other (Kartala) never succeeded in getting anything right. I saw similar double acts during my time as a missionary in Papula, New Guinea, in the 1970s. Two men would dress up as women and carry on hilarious conversations about life in the village. Everyone, including myself, managed to comprehend the fine nuances of the humor, since the situations they portrayed had an ageless quality about them. This same conflict is the basis of most comedy double acts right up to the present day, reflecting the power of the fool to succeed, again and again, against the odds.

God loves holy foolishness. The Old Testament contains many examples of this. It is instructive to find not just prophetic words but also prophetic *actions* common among the spiritual leaders of the people of Israel. There are also over 1,000 traditional tales and legends from Jewish sources. One Jewish legend relates to the way that Abram helped his father come to know more about God.

This is how it happened. Abram's father, Terah, worshiped idols. Not only did he bow down to them and offer them sacrifices, he also made them out of clay for others. He would make them just as the people wanted, custom made, and he hoped that his son would carry on the work.

One day Terah set off on a journey of several days. He put everything in Abram's hands, telling him the price of each of the idols, and saying he should sell as many as he could. Before long, a man came knocking at the door.

"What do you want?" Abram asked him.

"My wife sent me to buy some sort of a god. One that will watch over us and will not require too many sacrifices."

Abram nodded his head. "Tell me, how old are you?"

"Sixty," said the man.

"That's over 20,000 days," Abram laughed. "Would you really adore an idol that is just one day old?"

The old man was ashamed and went away empty-handed. The next day, a woman entered the house, carrying a bowl of flour. "Take this flour, please," she said to Abram, "and offer it up to one of the gods."

"What nonsense," cried Abram. "Is a piece of clay able to eat?"

He took a stick and smashed all the idols to pieces. He left only the largest figure in one piece. Then he placed the stick in its hand and the bowl of flour at its feet.

When Terah returned home, he was furious.

"Don't be angry, Father," Abram replied, "for a strange thing happened. A few days ago, a woman brought a bowl of flour as an offering to the gods. But as soon as they saw it, they began to quarrel. They all began to shout at once that they wanted to eat first, until the biggest of them took a stick and broke all the others to pieces. But as you can see, he did not eat the flour; if you wish, Father, I shall ask the god if he is hungry yet."

When he heard this, Terah shouted, "What is this you say? How could statues which I made with my own hands be *hungry* or *break each other*?"

"You see, Father," laughed Abram, "you yourself have said it. Your idols have eyes, but they do not see. They have ears, but they do not hear. Their noses can't smell, their mouths can't speak, their hands don't touch, their feet don't walk. They are not even the equals of man; they are only lumps of lifeless clay — and you would worship them as gods?"

Terah was silent...but he never, ever made an idol again.[4]

Noah is instructed to build the ark in the middle of the desert (Genesis 6:14). God calls Moses to lead the people of Israel (Exodus 3) in spite of (or maybe because of) the fact that he is

[4]Leo Paulat, *Jewish Tales: Eight Lights of the Hannukiya* (London: Beehive Books, 1986), 24.

"slow of speech and tongue" (Exodus 4:10). Gideon (Judges 7) tells the vast majority of his warriors to go home, leaving only three hundred. The weapons of victory are not swords or bows, but clay pots and flaming torches. The boy David defeats Goliath (1 Samuel 17) with the use of a simple sling. When David became King, he made up clever plans to get his own way (2 Samuel 11) which failed miserably. He used his human strength and not God's wisdom. Elijah is instructed to pour four large jars of water on the wood pile before God sets it on fire at the competition on Mount Carmel (1 Kings 18:33).

The prophets continually show holy foolishness in obedience to God's call. Jeremiah buys cloth to hide in a crack in the rock (Jeremiah 13:1-6) and retrieves it later. He goes to buy a new pot (Jeremiah 19) and then smashes it in front of the elders. Ezekiel eats a scroll in order to speak God's word (Ezekiel 3:1). He draws a map of the city on a brick and lies beside it (Ezekiel 4) for 390 days on his right side, then forty days on his left side. Later on (Ezekiel 5:1), he is told to shave his head and divide up the hair in thirds, again as a prophetic sign.

There are similar examples in the New Testament, but perhaps the first two chapters of 1 Corinthians sums up the call to be fools for Christ most completely.

Clown stories reappear in different forms from one country to another, and from one age to another. These folktales regularly contain descriptions of triumphant fools. The story may well be retold by different groups naming themselves as the heroes, but the actual conflicts and solutions will often remain very similar.

For example, the well-known plot of Shakespeare's *The Merchant of Venice* is a tale of cleverness against the treachery of the Jewish moneylender, Shylock. It is not common knowledge that the story has, in fact, a more ancient origin. It comes from a Jewish folktale in which the Jew is the hero and the rich Gentile merchant is the villain.[5]

[5]Phinhas Sadeh, "The Young Man and the Lawyer Who Was a Princess," *Jewish Folk Tales* (London: Collins, 1990), 277.

Another story told in many forms has been collected from Libya along the following lines:

In a certain town there lived a priest who hated the Jews. He persuaded the King to allow a public debate to determine whether or not they should be banished. When the King, under pressure, agreed, the Jews were very afraid. However, one of their number, the town fool, offered to represent them, arguing that even if he lost and was the first to be banished, he would not be much of a loss.

On the appointed day, the Priest suggested that they debate in sign language, to which the fool readily agreed.

The Priest began by taking an egg from his pocket. The fool responded by producing some salt.

Glaring angrily, the Priest then pointed both index fingers to the sky. The fool responded by pointing one finger upwards.

In a fury, the Priest took out a handful of barley and flung it on the ground. This time the fool opened his bag and let out a hen, who proceeded to eat up the grain.

"The debate is over," said the Priest. "I admit defeat."

The mystified King drew him aside and asked for an explanation.

"First I showed him an egg to illustrate that the Jews are two-faced; white on the outside and yellow on the inside. He replied with salt to say that they, on the contrary, are the salt of the earth.

"I then raised two fingers to show that the Jews serve two deities, God and mammon. He replied with one, to say they worship one God, Lord of heaven and earth.

"Finally I scattered seed to show that the Jews are scattered all over and will never unite. That's when he answered with the hen and allowed it to eat up the grain. This demonstrated the way the Jews' Messiah will gather up his people from all over the world."

At the same time, the Jews were rejoicing and listening to the fool's version of events.

"To tell the truth, I think the Priest must be out of his mind. When he got out an egg, I thought he was starting his lunch, so I offered him some salt, but he just put it away again. Then he got angry and pointed two fingers at me to poke my eyes out, so I showed him I could poke just as well. That made him so mad that he took some perfectly good seed and threw it away. I wasn't going to let it go to waste, so I let my hen eat it. Wouldn't you have done just the same?"[6]

In the Christian era, one of the Roman emperors passed a law compelling everyone to sacrifice to the Roman gods. One prominent Christian paid the clown Philemon to impersonate him and make the sacrifice in his place. Philemon agreed, treating it as a joke. At the last moment, he disclosed his true identity. He had fooled everyone and there was much laughter, but it was pointed out that he would still have to make the sacrifice. Philemon refused, saying he could not since, he, too, was a Christian. Even the Governor pleaded with him to change his mind, but without success, and so Philemon was executed. Rome lost a favorite clown, while the courageous fool gained a new title: Saint Philemon.

With the conversion of the Emperor Constantine in the fourth century A.D., Christianity became generally acceptable. Although this had many positive results, it had a detrimental effect on the visual arts in the church. Performing centers were closed and fools were moved out into the marketplaces, streets and fairs. The clowns began to team up with other wandering entertainers and became itinerant fools.

Each generation has a need of the clown-type figure to tell the truth with humor. In this way, societies may avoid taking themselves too seriously for their own good.

In the Middle Ages, the fool was again finding acceptance in some church circles. The chapel of the University of Barcelona in the twelfth century had a special trap door in the side of the sanctuary where the fool could enter.

---

[6]This Jewish story occurs in many forms. Details vary according to the country of origin.

These fools could often act as "divine interrupters." When they were involved in worship, they might encourage the congregation to rejoice or to listen with more attention to the preacher.

Eight hundred years ago, during the reign of King Henry I in England, the clown Rahare was well thought of in court circles. He was the most famous jester of his day. The King's son was drowned at sea, and the whole court moved into a time of mourning. The fool was given time off, and he decided to make a pilgrimage to Europe, which led him eventually to Rome. There were great dangers on the way, and Rahare became very sick. He made a vow to help the sick in England if God should spare him. He did gradually recover and made his first outing to St. Bartholomew's in Rome to thank God. That night he had a dream in which St. Bartholomew told him to go back to England, find a place called the smooth field and ask the King to give it to him as a site for a hospital and church.

Upon his return, Rahare found the place. It was a marshy area used by horse dealers and for markets. He appeared before the King and told him all that had happened to him. The King happily agreed to make the land available and to this day there is a hospital on this site, St. Bartholomew's of Smith Field.[7]

The Eastern Orthodox Church has valued the holy fool for many centuries, and the prophetic nature of this figure is recognized. Often these foolish prophets were hidden away from general view and known only to a few. Although the fool had the appearance of a madman, he had a secret life of prayer.

John Saward made a special study of such fools. He writes, "The fools for Christ's sake are men, made mad and merry by their faith in a God 'silly in the crib' and foolish on the cross, a

[7]S. E. Petts, *Modern Parables* (Kent: Henry Walker Ltd., 1971), 25.

God whose sage folly alone can save us from the raving lunacy of the princes of this age."[8]

This kind of folly has certain features:

1. It points to the future and recognizes that there is a kingdom beyond our present one.
2. It suggests pilgrimage and having no fixed home.
3. It represents association with strangers and outcasts.
4. It demonstrates alternative ways of living.
5. It is childlike.

A scholastic clown of God, Dr. Douglas Gifford, formerly of St. Andrews University on the east coast of Scotland, made a special study of the fool in the medieval period. He researched illuminated manuscripts from the eleventh to the fifteenth centuries and made some interesting discoveries.

Handwritten copies of Psalms 14 and 53 often contain an image of a fool or clown in the initial letter. By comparing these drawings, Gifford claims that the changes give us clues as to the place of the fool in society.[9]

The eleventh-century manuscripts portray the character as fool and prophet, while the later images are of the fun-loving jester with belled cap and beautiful costume. This suggests a development in the understanding of the clown's role at this time from truth-teller to joker.

In the fourteenth century, Nasr ed-Din was court jester to the Middle Eastern ruler Tamburlane. Though Tamburlane was a ruthless warrior, he was also a patron of literature and the arts.

One day Tamburlane caught sight of his reflection in a mirror and began to cry, because he saw how old and wrinkled he had become. Of course the rest of the court began crying also. After an hour or so, the Emperor stopped, dried his eyes, and got on with the rest of the day. The courtiers also ceased — everyone,

[8]John Saward, *Perfect Fools* (Oxford: Oxford University Press, 1978). Used by permission. (The book is now out of print.)

[9]D. Gifford, "Iconographical Notes Towards a Definition of the Medieval Fool,"*Journal of the Wadkig and Courtauld Institutes*, 37 (1974).

that is, except for Nasr ed-Din. In fact, Nasr was still howling the next morning when he came into the throne room. Tamburlane demanded to know why his jester was in such distress.

The clown replied, "Yesterday, when you looked in the mirror and saw what *you* looked like, you burst into tears, and when the mirror was taken away, you stopped crying. But I have to keep looking at your face *all the time*."

To everyone's relief, Tamburlane laughed — for had he not, it might have been the jester's last joke.

At the time of the Reformation in the sixteenth century, it is no surprise to find the jesters and clowns being regarded once more, with some justification, as frivolous people of no substance. As Christian buildings and theology were "tidied up," creative arts of all kinds were viewed with suspicion. This is not the whole story, however, as the Reformers themselves, and in particular, John Calvin, were never negative about creativity.

John Wilson, in his book on Calvin and the arts, draws attention to the ruling of Pope Gregory the Great towards the end of the sixth century. That was, "The picture is to the illiterate what the written word is to the educated."[10] And therefore, art thus became the picture book of the Bible. It was a natural step for new forms of drama to arise in the church. Mystery or miracle plays developed from the liturgy used in services. Additions were added to the text and verification crept in to intensify the story. Gradually, cycles of these plays began to appear, dealing with all the great stories of the Old and New Testaments. As the medieval church became more corrupt, so the arts became more secular. They had been the handmaid of the church, though this was due to economic, cultural and social factors rather than to a theological principle.[11]

Wilson continues to point out that John Calvin didn't condemn the arts at all; rather, he saw them as one of God's richest gifts to mankind. In *The Institutes of Christian Religion*, Calvin writes, "But as sculpture and painting are gifts of God,

---

[10]John Wilson, *One of the Richest Gifts* (Edinburgh: Hansel Press, 1981), 83.
[11]Ibid., 84.

what I insist on is that both shall be used purely and lawfully, that gifts which the Lord has bestowed upon us for his glory and our good shall not be abused."[12]

So, far from declaring the arts as unchristian, this Reformer wanted them to be fully used to glorify God. Christian artists were not to be limited to specifically religious themes. They were encouraged to seek the best and most appropriate ways of using these valuable gifts to edify others.

The plays of Shakespeare contain several notable clown characters, among them Bottom in *A Midsummer Night's Dream* and Lancelot Gobbo in *The Merchant of Venice*. The parts that Shakespeare wrote for these fools were small and for light relief. However, he did have problems with the popular performers who played these roles. As true clowns, they would, on occasion, delight the audience by ad-libbing and holding up the play with some comic song and dance routine.

The church has always counted among its members a few clown-type figures, such as John Ruysbroeck, a fourteenth-century divine from the Rhineland. Writing about the foolish joy of the Christian life, he refers to it as "spiritual inebriation." Two centuries later, Philip Neri, known as the "happy monk," used his joking and teasing as encouragement for his pupils. His playful style with those in his charge was legendary. He would go up to them at unexpected times, box their ears and say, "Be merry!"[13]

---

[12]John Calvin, Book 1, chap. 11 and chap. 12 in *The Institutes of Christian Religion*, trans. Henry Beveridge (n.p.: James Clark & Co. Ltd., 1962).
[13]More of his exploits are recorded in L. Bacci, *The Life of St. Philip Neri*, vol. 1 (London: Kegan Paul & Co., 1902), 194.

THREE-BALL JUGGLING

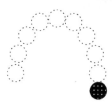

1. Forget all you already know about catching and throwing. Juggling is somewhat different. Begin with one ball. Hold hands at waist height. Keep as little movement in the arms as possible and throw the balls from hand to hand. The thrown ball should reach about head height.

DO THIS 10 TIMES.

2. With two balls, one in each hand, throw the right-hand ball as before. When it reaches maximum height, throw the left-hand ball under the falling ball. Catch the first ball in the right hand, and the second ball in the left hand. Remember to throw the second ball upward, under the path of the first ball.

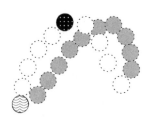

DO THIS 10 TIMES.

3. With three balls, two in the right hand and one in the left, throw as in **2** above. Hold the third ball in the palm of the right hand with the right little finger. This simply allows you to get used to holding three balls. The throwing is just as before.

4. Throw the third ball as follows: Throw the first ball as before, and the second underneath and upwards as it falls. *Now,* as the second ball falls toward the right hand, throw the *third* ball underneath and upwards on exactly the same path as the first ball. Catch the second ball in the right hand. One second later, catch the third ball in the left hand. STOP.

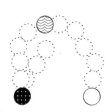

DO THIS 10 TIMES.

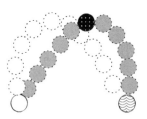

5. Now continue. As the third ball is falling toward the left hand, release (under and upwards) the ball held in that hand. On the same path as the second ball...and so on. Every time there is a ball in the air, it should be falling toward a hand with a ball in it. Simply move that hand-held ball under and throw, then catch the falling ball.

Now you are juggling!

Some tips:
Practice over a bed or sofa. You do not have to bend down so far to pick up any balls you drop. Concentrate always on the *throwing* of the ball. Count aloud a steady rhythm and throw in time to this. Catching is easy if the throws are in the right order, direction and strength. Practice regularly for short periods. Try not to tense up, as this makes control of the juggling difficult. Stay relaxed. Practice.

CHAPTER 3

A Brief History of Clowns (II)

Commedia dell'Arte

It would be fairer to speak of clown-type characters up till the eighteenth century. However, the development of the *commedia dell'arte* beyond its original homeland of Italy can be viewed as a major source of modern clowning.[1] The *commedia* has handed down over 800 scenarios, or *lazzi* (derived from the Italian word for "ribbon"). These could be developed in various ways, but the outlines and the endings were established. The word "lazzi" is also used to describe the outlining threads of a large work of tapestry that still needs areas to be filled in to finish the picture.

The commedia dell'arte developed from a simple, two-person sketch into extremely elaborate productions. In 1582, in Italy, the first record is found of a master/servant show that had the essence of this branch of the theatre.[2]

The aim was pure entertainment, and anything that could get a laugh was featured. This led to the inclusion of much side play and bawdy humor. It gave an excellent opportunity for the poor to laugh at the rich. Yet just as we saw with earlier forms of clown-type ministry, as the commedia dell'arte became more popular, the characters were acceptable to everyone as figures of fun.

Commedia dell'arte characters fall into two groups:

1. The Professionals

They symbolize the establishment and include Pantaloon (the rich miser), the Doctor (who is totally incompetent) and the Captain (the "brave" soldier who is afraid of everything).

[1]Raoul Sobel and David Francis, *Chaplin: Genesis of a Clown* (London: Quartet Books, 1979), includes some useful information on commedia dell'arte.

[2]Ferruveccio Solieri, *Commedia Dell'Arte Portraits* (A one-man show performed live by Ferruveccio Solieri, in Glasgow, Scotland, 1993).

Pantaloon is an elderly, greedy merchant, usually infatuated with a much younger woman. He tries to use his wealth and position to impress her, but continually fails. Extremely fat and slow-moving, he usually wears a brown mask over his eyes and nose and dresses in dark colors.

The Doctor, or Astrologer, is a close friend of Pantaloon. He might also be a lawyer or a professor, pedantic in style and totally incompetent. He tries to impress others by using long words and Latin phrases, always in the wrong context. He usually carries a book, which he consults grandly on every possible occasion. His half mask is black and might have a stubby beard attached.

The third character of the professional group is *the Captain*. He boasts of his conquests, both military and romantic, but is at heart a coward. Though he might carry a long sword, he is never able to draw it. Though he swaggers about confidently in fine silk clothes, he is terrified of everything. If someone sneezes, he hides. If he sees an ant, he runs away. This person might also be an Admiral who, of course, is seasick at the sight of water. His mask is flesh colored, with a bristling mustache and a huge nose.

2. The Servants

They are the younger and more attractive characters. Brighello, Pedroline, Pierrot and Pulcinello represent clown wisdom and cleverness in the face of adversity. The general name for these comic hired hands is *zanni*.

Brighello is usually employed by a very rich master, and he is used as a go-between in amorous adventure. He is an ambivalent chap — at times a thug and a thief, but also charming, able to play the guitar well and sing beautifully. He is very unpredictable, unlike most of the other characters. His half mask is yellow with a long, hooked nose.

Pedroline, the brother of Brighello, is always in love. He is extremely sensitive and far too shy to ever let his true emotions be known. He is very naive and believes everything he is told without question. This is the original character behind the

Pierrot. Though Pierrot lost some of Pedroline's simplicity, he gained more in pathos. There are times when this character, though deeply in love, never approaches his beloved for fear of being rejected. Traditionally, he wore no mask but covered his face in white flour. This same use of the white face surfaces in the early silent movies, with the same type of characters.

Pulcinello is the oldest of the servants. He is aggressive, energetic and wears a hawk-like expression. He is apt to scream or crow to draw attention to himself.

The most famous of the zanni is *Arlecchino,* or *Harlequin*. Previously, he was a simpleton who was forever in love. He was continually cuffed and corrected by the other players. In the modern cartoons the harlequin-type character never gets hurt and always bounces back up again. He is agile and acrobatic. Over time, his character has developed, and he has become more cunning — a greedy rogue. His traditional costume consists of many different colored triangles. These give the impression of patches and are intended to represent poverty. His half mask is often dark brown with a smile fixed upon it.

Arlecchino has a female counterpart in *Columbine*. Worldly wise and witty, she acts as a go-between. She has various liaisons herself and always comes off best from any love affair she enters into, yet she is really in love with Arlecchino.

While some of the individuals in the commedia didn't deviate from the standard performance, others began to develop along their own lines.

Pulcinello became popular in England as a puppet, and the *Punch and Judy* shows were staged at seaside resorts. Punch was an unattractive person who always seemed to get away with his wrongdoing. Many of the other puppets were echoes of the commedia dell'arte, but the show could be quickly and easily presented by only one or two people.

Pierrots also became popular as performing groups at seaside resorts, though other characters gradually died out in most parts of Europe. The Pierrot shows would include groups of musicians all dressed in loose white costumes with large black or red pompoms attached. These were much more like variety shows in fancy dress than any kind of clown presentation, and in time, the costumes were discarded. When the Pierrot shows lost their popularity, individual performers adapted material for the circus, street fairs and festivals.

There are difficulties today for touring groups for the commedia dell'arte, due to the specialized nature of the material. I have seen mime artists Ferruccio Solieri (Italy), Bill Angel (Holland) and Peri Aston (London) give demonstrations of the commedia characters. They are very interesting as far as the history of theatre is concerned. However, since the comedy depends so heavily upon interaction, this is not the ideal way of presenting the heart of the commedia. The Punch and Judy show, for all its limitations, does convey more of the spirit of the original presentations.

Traveling circus groups always enlisted the help of clowns during performances. The main acts needed time to change their costumes, and it was most natural to use clowns to fill in between these spots. One great advantage was that the clown was able to ad-lib, e.g., to lengthen a particular piece and develop it on the spot should the need arise. One of the greatest arts of the clown became the ability to give the impression of ad-libbing when in fact the whole piece had been carefully sculpted beforehand over the course of many performances.

Some clowns developed into individual stars, such as Grimaldi. At the height of Grimaldi's success, the story is told of a very depressed man who visited the doctor, asking for help with his melancholia.

"You should go and see Grimaldi. He will cheer you up," advised the doctor.

"But I *am* Grimaldi," replied his patient.

The Swiss clown Grock, a large, clumsy Auguste, moved from circus to stage with his clown act. He attempted to play many musical instruments, but he failed at each one — except for a tiny violin. This he was able to play beautifully.

In the United Kingdom, Coco the clown became the main

attraction in the circus and fascinated a whole generation with his collapsing clown car. The highly polished car would be driven into the ring. The doors, failing to close, eventually came off completely. Then the radiator would "explode" dramatically, the hood and trunk flying open and other parts falling off the structure. Even after the apparent destruction of the car, it was amazingly still able to be driven out of the circus ring.

The silent films provided a natural medium for mime and acrobatic clowning. There is no doubt that Charlie Chaplin, Harold Lloyd and Buster Keaton were direct descendants of the commedia dell'arte tradition. Some of their material can be traced back to the original lazzi of the eighteenth century. As with all clowning, the real delight was found in the creative use of the well-worn plot outline.

The television has proved to be an unfriendly medium for circus skills in general and clowns in particular. One of the most significant aspects of clowning is the ability to involve the audience and draw out reaction. Television as a medium is not suited for such a high level of concentrated involvement. The possibility of distraction is high, and timing is precisely limited to the second. There is little chance of drawing an audience into the imaginary world of the gentle clown. There are, of course, notable exceptions, but these tend to be humorous mime artists as often as they are true clowns.

A recent survey[3] of evangelistic methods in the United Kingdom has found that a significant number of people mentioned live performance in a Christian context as being influential in their coming to faith in Christ, while relatively few referred to films and television. The conclusion of this report is that much more attention and support should be given to live visual arts performances.

The survey concludes its chapter on the media as follows:

> This survey suggests that if the church wishes to evangelize through the media, the electronic means are less effective than others. Support should there-

[3]J. Finney, *Finding Faith Today: How Does It Happen?* (Westlea, Swindon: Bible Society, 1992).

fore be given to live drama, literature, and music at least as much as to TV and radio.

Some churches channel their resources toward electronic rather than "live" presentations: the survey suggests this may be a mistake. The size of audience for the "live" may be only a tiny fraction of that for the electronic media but appears to have a greater effect.[4]

Floyd Shaffer says, "History shows that clowns have not been seen so much as performers, but rather as those who are expected to create an environment in which things can happen."

The church "environment" is again being enriched by those seeking to be happily foolish in the service of God. For a time, at least in our day, clowns are becoming *persona grata* in the assemblies of God's people.

---

[4]J. Finney, *Finding Faith Today: How Does It Happen?* (Westlea, Swindon: Bible Society, 1992).

MASKS

Purchase an inexpensive basic plastic mask from a toy or craft store. Either a clear mask or a fairly naturalistic one will work well.

1. Cover the mask with a thin covering of Vaseline.

2. Now prepare a mixture of wallpaper paste and water and tear sheets of newspaper into strips of approximately 1" x 6". Dip the strips in the paste mixture and cover most of the mask as shown.

3. When the mask is covered with one layer of paper, continue to add more and more strips to build up the thickness.

4. As the thickness is being built up, certain features such as the nose, eyebrows and cheeks can be reshaped.

5. Finally, allow the mask to dry for twenty-four hours, then paint with appropriate colors. Remove the paper mask from the base and add cord elastic as shown.

SOME CHARACTER MASKS

Pantaloon

The Doctor

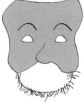

The Captain

Arlecchino

Brighello

Masks

CHAPTER 4

The Clown as Child

Every clown has his or her own unique approach. These range from the loud, intrusive characters so beloved of slapstick sketches in the circus, to the quiet, withdrawn mime of the classic theatre. The word "clown" has a variety of meanings. It comes from a Scandinavian word meaning a clod or a lump of earth, and also a country bumpkin. It may refer to a clumsy person or someone who is deliberately funny. It is not too surprising that the church has found it difficult to come to terms with such an ambivalent character.

Perhaps the best way forward is for us to consider what is distinctive about Christian clowns and fools.

There are few specific references to the fool in the Scriptures. These occur mainly in the Psalms and Paul's first letter to Corinth, but Jesus frequently refers to the childlike nature of faith.[1] This gives us some clues as to the nature of clown ministry. Not everything a child does is good, and we need to distinguish between childlikeness and childishness. The latter can be seen as a form of selfishness; the natural, self-centered world view of the young has many unattractive features. However, some of the characteristics of childlikeness are strikingly similar to the foolish clown. One definition of the Christian clown is the "child of God."

1. Enthusiasm

This word comes from a compound Greek word, *enthusios,* which literally means "in God." There is little that can be achieved without enthusiasm. Young children often show great ability to show their feelings of delight. They have the ability to be caught up in a game or pursuit to the exclusion of all else. While their enthusiasm may not be of long duration, it is often

[1]Luke 18:17, Matt. 18:2.

completely absorbing. Enthusiasm may be misplaced, but it can also be very life-affirming.

My wife's paternal grandmother was a great enthusiast. She loved her family dearly and used to be greatly elated when she learned that any of them were to visit her home. She would tell all her neighbors and friends about it for days in advance of their visits. On at least two occasions, she fell over in her excitement when rushing to greet her visitors.

2. Joy

Enjoyment is a state of delight more often found among children and clowns than in grown -ups.

The book *Tom Sawyer* by Mark Twain opens with a chapter of Tom's cleverness. He has been forced to whitewash a fence as a punishment from his Aunt Polly. By using his wits, Tom tricks his friends, one after another, into doing the work for him. Not just that, he also manages to get them to pay for the privilege with toys and food. By the end of chapter one, Tom, the hero, has fooled his friends and has gotten out of painting the fence.[2] Initially, Tom's friends seem to have been duped. It appears that they have lost out to a smarter kid. There is another way to look at this, however, since Tom had to work very hard to convince his friends to work for him. They, on the other hand, found joy and pleasure. Tom gave them a "game" of painting the fence, and they went home fulfilled and happy. Of course, if Tom's friends were told of his scheme later in the day, this would take away some of their joy, and cynicism might begin to get a hold on their future relationships with him.

Joy can take on various forms. Jean Vanier recounts a creative way of ending a mealtime within a community when oranges were part of the meal. It was not uncommon for the bits of peel to be playfully thrown across the table.[3]

Our family discovered, quite spontaneously, a similar hilarious game at a recent evening meal. I arrived late and

[2]Mark Twain, *The Adventures of Tom Sawyer* (New York: Grosset and Dunlop Inc., 1946).

[3]Jean Vanier, *Community and Growth* (London: D.L.T., 1979), 241.

found my seat taken by my youngest son. Instead of reacting to this, I took my youngest son's seat and began to act out his mannerisms and conversation. The rest of the family quickly joined in changing seats and role-playing each other in turn. It was a time of joyous and therapeutic laughter.

3. Simplicity

As the old Shaker hymn says, "'Tis a gift to be simple." Children often have amazingly profound insights because of this. The composer Mozart, when he was four years old, was asked how he managed to compose such wonderful music. His reply is said to have been, "I just put together little notes that like each other."

Complicated language may often be a shield, defense or a sign of someone showing off. I recall being very impressed upon learning from a German theologian that Mark's gospel was "a concatenation of parenetic pericopae." It was disappointing to find out that this simply meant a series of little stories for teaching. There is a natural desire in adults to explain and make more obvious that which even a child can see. Simplicity is a gift, but it can and should be cultivated by all those seeking to be foolish for the Lord.

The best-selling book *All I Really Need to Know I Learned in Kindergarten* by Robert Fulghum was recommended at the first International Clown Summit here in Scotland as essential reading for all clowns, by one of Ringling's Clown College teachers. This includes an introductory chapter on how to live life to the fullest. It includes such helpful advice as "Take a nap each afternoon." "Put things back where you find them." "Warm cookies and cold milk are good for you."

4. Living for the Moment

Children know instinctively that you can't change the past, but you can ruin a perfectly good present by worrying about the future. This quality can also be found in the spiritual writings of the Middle Ages. Brother Lawrence, a monk who spent most of his life in prayer and working in the monastery kitchen, became famous for a little book on living each moment for God.[4] While children may not fully articulate or even hold such views, the resulting simplicity has a childlike quality to it. The negative side of this may be seen when parents begin to give in to their children's desire to have everything *now*.

5. Truthfulness

Young children do not know what *not* to say. The trouble of speaking without thinking, as adults find out much to their embarrassment, is that children may say what they really think. In the fairy tale *The Emperor's New Clothes*, it is the child who opens his mouth and speaks the truth that everyone else was afraid to tell. He breaks through all the pretense and lies and proclaims in true clown style, "He's got nothing on!"

When our youngest son was five years old, he often felt the need for plenty of attention at bedtime. One night he called out from his bedroom in great distress. We went to see what was wrong, and he grabbed his throat, moaning, "Oh, it's so sore."

His mother went off to get some medicine and put just the tiniest drop onto a spoon. He looked up just before taking it, saying "It won't hurt if you're just pretending, will it?"

Communicating truth may not always be straightforward. We need to beware of confusion, especially in cross-cultural situations. During the time of the British rule in India, court cases often required interpreters. A British judge suspicious of a particular witness said to the interpreter, "Tell the witness, *'There is no need for unnecessary lies.'* " The interpreter translated this for the man as, "The judge is saying, *'Tell lies only when necessary.'* "

6. Vulnerability

Children are easily hurt, physically and emotionally. Openness and gentleness are natural attributes which can be quickly lost. Adults are at first seen, as the giants in fairy tales show us, as strong, rich and powerful. They can be fearsome

[4]Brother Lawrence, *The Practice of the Presence of God* (Mt. Vernon, NY: Peter Pauper Press, 1963).

figures, though most children will have begun life with at least some benevolent adult protectors.

As children begin to identify those who are skilled and attractive in their peer group, they also discover those who are different. Those who are weak or unusual are often sidelined and isolated by others.

At school, when children are playing team games, the team leaders are often given the choice of who will be on their team. This can be a painful experience for the less able, as it becomes obvious that they are going to be picked last. One episode of the TV program *The Wonder Years*, a series about growing up in the 1960s, dealt with this issue in a beautiful way. The hero, uncomfortable at being put in the position of having to choose a team, decided to pick all those others considered useless. His team lost the game, but won a victory of another kind.

There is still another way of choosing teams that shows how "clown thinking" can be applied. This is used in parts of Russia and overcomes some of the difficulty. This is how it works: The children choose a partner of roughly the same height and they decide together on two words which are closely related, such as door and wall or forest and river. They will take one of these names each. The pair then goes to the leader and asks the question, "Which do you want — the door or the wall?" The result is two fairly equal teams and no embarrassed children waiting to be picked.

A further example of a sense of community in children was related to me by a lady who had taught Inuit children in the far north of Canada. She found it very hard to motivate her pupils, and in an effort to encourage them to work harder, she offered a prize for the best piece of homework handed in next day. She was shocked and angry when she found the children handed in identical answers obviously copied from one common source. The children were equally surprised by her reaction. "But whoever wins the prize would share it with all the others anyway, and none of us wanted our classmates to feel less clever, so we all did the assignment together," they told her. As a result, she considered how the community of children might react when teaching her following lessons, and she creatively used this understanding for the good of all, including herself.

7. Discovery

Some Japanese friends shared with me the following examples of how well that country understands the need for children to make their own discoveries, especially in the natural world. In a densely populated country, it takes a great deal of planning to allow each child the special privilege of finding natural objects.

In the autumn, classes of children are taken to the forests, in strict rotation, for an hour of chestnut collecting. A woodsman waits and watches each group, and as soon as the children leave and before the next group arrives, he scatters a fresh supply of chestnuts under the trees for the next class to find. I am told he has a hut to rest in, and behind the hut are boxes of chestnuts labeled "Imported From China."

In the summer, the children have a similar "collecting hour" on the beach, where they look for edible shellfish in the shallow waters. The beach is sectioned off with ropes and pegs so that several groups can search at the same time. When the hour is almost up, it might be that only one or two children will have found anything worth keeping. So, to avoid disappointment, a helper arrives and tips a box of shellfish into the shallows for the children to pick up and "find." No one goes home empty handed.

I showed a Soma[5] cube to Seishiro Yuasa, a Japanese friend of mine who teaches kindergarten. It consists of seven irregular pieces which may be formed into various shapes and patterns, but usually start out as a cube. After the pieces have been taken apart, it is quite a challenge to reassemble the original cube. Yuasa told me he would put the separate pieces into the kindergarten play box and let the children play with the shapes without telling them that it was possible for them to make a cube shape.

[5]Martin Gardner, "The Soma Cube," chap. 6 in *More Mathematical Puzzles and Diversions* (New York: Penguin Books, 1962).

Then he told me, "One day maybe in two weeks or two years, someone may discover without help the wonderful cube."

8. Creativity

Children find much joy in creating and discovering. To make something out of almost nothing has universal appeal to those with the heart of a child. It is not uncommon to find a very young child more interested in the wrapping paper, box and bow than in the present carefully chosen by the parents. Adults have learned to value things according to their monetary value. Toys are designed today with the parent in mind just as much as the child. There is little real understanding of the need to encourage creativity.

The world of the child (and the clown) has different values and priorities than that of the adult world. One cold summer day (there are many of those in Scotland) when I was three years old, I remember my godfather insisting that I paddle in the pool because he had already paid for me to do so. I did go into the water, but only to make him happy.

Jesus taught about the need we all have to become like children — that is, childlike but not childish.[6] Only the children of God will have a place in the kingdom. It will be a country without adults. Richard Wurmbrand, a pastor from Russia who has suffered severe persecution for his faith, points out that only the children of Israel came out of captivity in Egypt. Evidently, to children at least, the adults were left behind. On hearing this, one child added, "Yes, and Jesus is coming back with his arms full of toys."

The kingdom is also for the weak, the poor and the hurt, a place for parties and celebration, for stillness and stories.

The Christian clown is able to bring enthusiasm, joy, creativity and the other aforementioned characteristics to the attention of his or her audience. This can never be aggressive and requires much patience. It takes a long time to become young. This knowledge will bring a tolerance toward others and

[6]John 3:3; Luke 18:16.

an understanding that competitiveness can have a destructive effect on community. The call to become children is simply a call to become what God wants us to be. For those called to be clowns, this means becoming the person we were made to be all of the time and not only in costume.

It is possible and indeed necessary to learn from others without copying them; however, I have found performing artists to be very gracious people, ready to share and encourage others who have a genuine interest and are willing to apply themselves and practice skills. In my experience, I have found that in general, non-Christian performers are more relaxed and ready to share their gifts and skills with other artists than Christian artists. This may be due to the church's ambivalent attitude toward the arts, and I do notice that this is changing as more Christians become involved. I am finding it less necessary to paint Christian symbols on my made-up clown face, though I still wear the words "Jesus Lives" on the back of my clown costume. My new character has a small golden cross on rainbow braces, but it is only visible if you know where to look.

THE ORANGE-SKINNED MONKEY

1. Cut skin as shown.

2. Remove peel.

3. Cut spiral in base.

4.

5. Ease orange carefully out of its skin.

6. Eat the orange.

7.

Place the monkey over the neck of a bottle.

Leave for several days and the head will come up into position.

CHAPTER 5

Clown Costumes and Makeup

As we have already seen, clowns vary in action and appearance, from the rags and simple clothes of the early fool, to the fancy jester's costumes of the Middle Ages. In more recent times, the word "clown" has become synonymous with the circus clown. Some of these characters can be traced to the commedia dell'arte. While the personality types are not clearly defined in the modern circus, the routines still owe a great deal to the routines of the commedia.

There are three main clown types that have established themselves in the twentieth-century circus:

1. The Neat Whiteface Clown

This clown is usually tall, elegant and musical, traditionally playing the clarinet and guitar. He or she is a bossy and serious individual with little sense of humor, in whose presence everyone must behave. Everything has to be done exactly as he or she wants.

His costume is beautifully elaborate, usually multicolored with sequins, and he never, ever gets dirty, no matter how much mess is made by others. He loves to direct and order others around, but has a somewhat distant and unattractive temperament. He is an authority figure who always ends up the butt of the other clowns' jokes. Maybe we see in him the father figure, the boss at the office, the official who wants to have his own way, no matter what others think.

His makeup usually consists of a white face (sometimes also neck and ears), with strong, simple lines of black around the eyebrows or mouth. Though most Whiteface clowns use very little makeup or color, the eyebrow lines can be so distinctive that they alone may identify a famous clown.

It is sometimes the custom to paint the outer rim of the ear red, but the significance of this seems to have been lost in the mist of time.

2. The Auguste Clown

His name comes from the German word for clumsy. He is the foil of the Whiteface, often dropping things, making a mess, or generally causing confusion. For all the apparent animosity between the two, they clearly need each other and there are definite limits to the relationship. It is not dissimilar to the relationship between the master and servant of the commedia dell'arte.

He usually wears a brightly colored, oversize coat. It has deep pockets from which he can produce the most unlikely objects, from chickens to parasols. He often sports large clown shoes, a wide tie and an orange wig.

The Auguste tries very hard to please the Whiteface, but always ends up on the wrong end of things. For example, if he should plan to throw a custard pie[1] at the Whiteface clown, it will almost certainly end up on his own face.

The Auguste is a skilled performer also, but this is less obvious to the audience. Often he will be able to juggle unusual objects and walk the slack rope (with many wobbles, to keep up the impression of his clumsiness).

3. The Tramp Clown

This type of clown appeared in the circus ring in the mid-twentieth century. The first Tramp clown to gain wide recognition was an American named Emmet Kelly. Kelly was famous for his sad countenance and his apparent unawareness of his surroundings. One of his most loved exploits was when he would enter the circus tent with a broom and begin to sweep up. He would then take a seat in the audience, apparently waiting for the next act, remove a cabbage wrapped in newspaper from

[1]The current trend is to use a paper plate with a large amount of shaving cream on it.

a large pocket, and begin to eat, offering leaves to others around him so that they might share in his picnic. He would be very sad should anyone not accept.

Recently I saw a wonderful clown called Pins, whose costume was a tweed suit that had seen better days. It was cut and torn in countless places — almost in rags, but everything was held together by hundreds and hundreds of safety pins.

It is perhaps right to regard the European clown as yet another type. The European clowns are somewhat similar to the Tramp clowns in that they generally dress in less outlandish costumes. They wear less makeup than traditional circus clowns, and if they use a false nose, it is usually small. These clowns concentrate on touching the emotions rather than on slapstick and tumbling skills. They are often able to work as solo performers and have extremely attractive personalities. In Eastern Europe, clowns are rightly regarded as true artists and are held in high regard.

While these main categories are well-established in classical circus and theatre, the situation has changed today. Now that clowns have moved back onto the streets and into churches, widening their performing repertoire, distinctions are less clear.

The emphasis now is not so much on finding a clown type as it is on being a consistent personality. For example, in the relationship between the Whiteface and the Auguste, should the Auguste actually *appear* to be more skillful than the Whiteface, a whole range of clown possibilities is lost. The interaction has parallels which go right back to earliest times as authority is challenged by the courageous fool.

Many cultures have used ways of painting the face white as a sign of their respect or emotion to the rites of passage.

The white face is a symbol of death in many cultures and is commonly used in festivals of celebration also. From personal experience and conversations with people from other cultures, I have found that the custom of covering the face with clay and white ashes as a mark of mourning is widespread. In Zambia, however, the leaders of the Bemba people traditionally paint their faces white as a sign of celebration. The leader of leaders is permitted to add red marks to the white.

STRING GAME RELEASE

1.

2.

3.

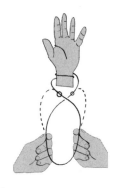

4.

5.

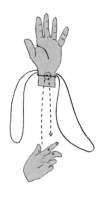

6.

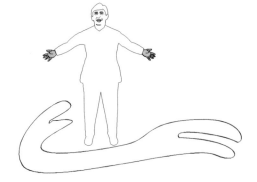

Finding a Clown Character

Since no two people are alike, no two clowns will be either. This uniqueness of the individual is the most important consideration for novice clowns. It is quite natural to begin by imitating the clown you admire most. Most clowns start out this way. They try to find matching clothing, will put on makeup in a similar style, and practice the same routines. There is no harm beginning this way, but there is a kind of copyright in clown makeup that is worth respecting. You can, in due course, submit your own clown "face" for registration.

Your first attempts at applying clown makeup are unlikely to produce a stable pattern. Do not worry about this. Just persevere and concentrate on keeping the design simple. It is not a good idea to have someone else put on your makeup for you unless they are willing and able to do it every single time you perform. With practice, it becomes fairly easy to do. Applying makeup also provides an opportunity for a quiet time of preparation before performance.

There are two main types of makeup generally available today. Both are available in a wide range of colors.

1. Water-based Makeup

This is very quick and easy to apply and the colors are strong. The widely available face paints for children have the advantage of being cheap, but the colors are not very strong or long-lasting. Thus, though good-quality makeup might originally appear expensive, if you use it properly, it will last a long time and give much better results. If you have sensitive skin, this is the best kind to begin experimenting with.

2. Oil-based Makeup

This is the traditional "grease paint." It is characterized by good, strong colors. The makeup tends to last longer and is not easily smudged. It can take much longer to remove, however, and this can be a great disadvantage if quick change is desirable.

Putting on makeup is an art form in itself. Although it may best be learned from theatrical sources, following are some hints on how to put on an "acceptable" clown face.

Allow plenty of time to put on makeup and apply one color at a time. Dust down with talcum powder at each stage. I use a small sock full of powder and knotted at the opening, but you can, of course, use a powder puff. The loose powder should be carefully brushed away and the face gently pressed with a damp cloth. This brings out the full colors and also helps to fix the makeup firmly.

Oil-based makeup will last for several hours without further attention, no matter how hot or wet you get.

Finding the best shapes and pattern for your clown face takes time. Do remember that the makeup is not so much a mask to hide behind as it is a way of showing your facial expressions more clearly.

Begin by looking at your face in a mirror. Smile, frown, wink and generally move your face as much as you can. You will notice that some parts of the face remain fairly static (the nose), while others can move a great deal (the mouth and eyebrows). Try marking the points of greatest movements with lines of color to make them even more obvious. The nasal labial folds (a fancy way of describing the lines formed by the bottom of the cheeks) can give good lines for mouth makeup. Static points can also be highlighted to good effect and help to give reference points to the more mobile features.

As a broad rule, use no more than three colors on a white background. You may find that one or two colors are even more effective. Only choose one or two features to highlight, and avoid making too many shapes. Too much fine detail tends to confuse and distort the face when seen from far away. It is wise to keep makeup away from the eyes until you become proficient at applying it. Even a small amount can be extremely difficult to remove without affecting the eyes.

Clown costumes may be purchased from stores and theatrical suppliers, but there are great advantages to finding or making your own outfit. Look for brightly colored shirts, ties and jackets. If you are tall, then vertical stripes will emphasize your height. On the other hand, baggy and loose clothing with large shoes often suit small-framed clowns. Again, some candid observation of your body size and shape in the mirror might give some ideas as to the sort of costume that would be best. The most effective clown is one who is recognizable as the same character, even when he has lost some of his props and/or clothes. Be creative.

It is wise to keep outfits simple so it is easy to change into and out of costume. I can change into my present costume in about thirty seconds. This is very useful when changing rooms are nonexistent. The unique clown in us (and remember, again, *no one* else is like us) can become very effective in ministry when the same "faithful" character is found after the makeup is removed. It may be that the Christian clown comes to the point of using less and less makeup as the holy fool shines through the skin. This is why I do not regard makeup as a way of hiding the person. Bill Angel,[1] a friend of mine, leads seminars on maskwork. He makes the point that the mask does not conceal the wearer, rather, it actually helps us to see his or her whole body.

The clown face may be seen as a way of removing the mask worn for everyday relationships at home and work. There are some parallels here with the expression Paul uses in Romans relating to being baptized into the death of Christ.[2]

Very young children like clowns, or are at least neutral in their responses. Sometimes, however, children around age four can be very nervous and even terrified by clowns. It may be that they recognize a link between the white face and the fact of death. This universal symbol has lost its significance to most adults, but there seems to be a natural awareness of this among the young. In my experience, most children over the age of five become clown-friendly once again.

[1]Bill Angel is a drama teacher and performing artist based in London. Bill also works for Dutch TV on a regular basis.
[2]Rom. 6:4.

HANKY MOUSE

Use a large white square of material.

1. Fold in half, then fold sides in at the lines.

2. Now begin to roll up from the bottom...

3. ...to look like this.

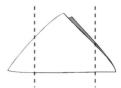

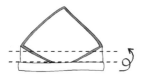

4. Turn over.

5. Fold in sides to overlays as follows, then turn over.

6. Fold up once...

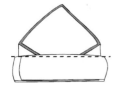

7. ...like this.

8. Now tuck the double corner into the center.

9. From the bottom, begin to open the hanky with a rolling movement.

10. Keep on going until...

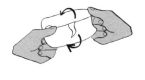

11. ...two loose ends appear.

12. Stretch one end open, like this...

...and knot to give the head and ears.

13. The other end is the tail.

14. Hold mouse as shown and stroke with right hand.

15. Mouse jumps forward.

16. Movement is controlled by the left middle finger. The source of the movement is hidden by the cover of the right hand so the mouse appears to jump by itself.

CHAPTER 7

Take Me to Your Leader

In any new form of ministry, misunderstandings can easily arise. It is therefore important to get permission to clown around in churches. Any positive effects can be completely lost if the performers are not in sympathy with the vision that the leaders of the local church have. Christian clowns involved in worship and outreach need to be fully aware of the expectations of others.

Once in our early days as clowns, our troupe had prepared a thoughtful presentation on life and death. The pastor introduced us as "silly clowns" and encouraged the teenage audience to laugh as much as they liked. When we finished, there was an embarrassed silence and a very confused audience. On this occasion, every detail of the routines we had planned worked perfectly, but we failed to communicate the message we intended due to false expectations.

It is vital to make sure that the purpose of the meeting is clearly understood and agreed upon in advance. Even when this is done, there will be a need to adapt and change material on short notice. Even very simple and basic ideas can have a powerful effect if they are shared at the right time.

Since there is such a variety of clown types and performances, it is very important to have contact with the leaders of the meeting beforehand. When you determine the goals and style of the meeting, you are then able to select the most appropriate material and presentation. It will also help if you have contact with other Christian clowns whose styles and talents differ from yours. Then, if a particular request does not seem to be in tune with your style or ability, you may be able to recommend another group of clowns who may be more suitable for the job.

Most of the invitations I receive come from people who have seen me perform or who have had contact with someone who has recommended me. The fact that I am in touch with other clowns and recommend them for particular work also means they often put people in touch with me if there is a request they feel unable to fulfill for whatever reason. This is an informal network, but it gives a great strength and broad base for ministry.

Christian clowns will add to what is already happening in the church, even if this means a radical challenge to the status quo. The clown should not be *the* leader of the church. He is there to comment on or reflect the congregation's attitude back to them. The clown is not against tradition, but helps the church rediscover a proper attitude about its past.

It is helpful to share with the church leaders some of the tradition of the fool for Christ, though I always add that tradition on its own is not a good enough reason for doing anything. The following story illustrates this.

A young girl used to enjoy watching her mother prepare Sunday dinner. Every Sunday, her mother would prepare a leg of lamb in the same way. Having basted it, she would then cut the end off the bone with an axe just before putting it into the oven.

So in due course, when the girl grew up and got married, she, too, prepared a leg of lamb for Sunday dinner in exactly the same way.

One day, when her husband was watching her cook, he asked, "Why do you cut the end off the bone?"

His wife thought for a moment, then said, "I don't know, but I'll ask my mother next week when she visits us."

Her mother visited the next week and her daughter asked, "Mum, remember how you used to prepare the Sunday leg of lamb?"

"Yes, dear, what about it?" her mother asked.

"Well, I've forgotten why it is that you cut the end off of it before putting it in the oven." Her mother laughed, "Oh, don't you remember? Our oven was so small that we couldn't get it in otherwise."

In a church that is not familiar with clown ministry, I find it helpful to make some explanation beforehand. Sometimes I use stories of the prophets. At other times, I apply my clown makeup in front of the audience. I do this as a tape of a song I wrote, "I'd Like to Be a Clown," plays in the background, or as I tell "Truth and Parable" (page 7), a story which involves the actual application of clown makeup. An alternative to putting on the actual clown face is to use a large picture with flaps that fold over[1] to show the different stages of clown makeup.

Another good story which will help prepare a congregation for clowns inside the church building is *The Clown of God*.[2]

A young boy, Giovanni, had a very special gift of juggling. He became famous for it, and one day two Franciscan brothers saw him perform. They approached him and said, "Our founder, Brother Francis, says that everything sings of the glory of God — why, even your juggling," said one of the brothers.

"That's well and good for you, but I only juggle to make men smile and laugh," Giovanni said.

"It's the same thing," said the brothers. "If you give happiness to people, you give glory to God as well."

"If you say so...but I must be off," responded the juggler.

Many years later, Giovanni, by then an old man, found himself no longer able to juggle so well, no longer the center of others' admiration.

Sheltering in a large church one night, he noticed a large painting of Mary and the baby Jesus, both looking sad. Giovanni longed to cheer them up. He took out his juggling balls and attempted his special trick, juggling six colored balls, when suddenly his old heart stopped and he fell to the floor, dead. Two brothers came rushing into the church to see what was happening. They looked at the old juggler lying on the floor and remembered that they had met once before. They saw all

[1]For the principles of the folding picture see "The Butterfly Story" on page 83.
[2]One version is told in Tomie De Paola's *The Clown of God* (New York: Harcourt Brace Jovonovich, 1978). The story is also known as *The Juggler of God* (or *The Juggler of Notre Dame*).

his juggling balls there, save one. As they looked around, they noticed the painting. Mary and Jesus were no longer sad — both were smiling. They gasped in delight as they saw the child cradling a beautiful yellow orb in his hand.

While it is vital to have good communication with church leaders and those in authority, we cannot allow others to dictate the way we are to behave. This would simply be to act "as if" we were clowns. It is important to be able to turn down invitations.

Laurens Van Der Post, the traveler and author, records how trade was allowed in sixteenth-century Japan on certain conditions:

> The Dutch established what they called a "factory" at Doshuima, an island off Nagasaki, and were allowed a strictly limited number of ships to Japan, but only on the condition that twice a year, the commander of the factory and his principal officers allowed themselves to be paraded through the streets of Yedo (as Tokyo was then called) dressed like clowns and other comic figures and generally subjecting themselves to public humiliation. Above all, once a year they had to trample on a wooden cross in front of a Japanese official. Yet for centuries, the material gain was thought well worth the depravity implied in the process...[3]

---

[3]Laurens Van Der Post, *Yet Being Someone Other* (London: Hogarth Press, 1983), 65.

IMPOSSIBLE BALANCE

The object pictured below is made from one piece of wood about 2" x 1". When people are asked to balance it upon one finger, they find this difficult, if not impossible.

Sometimes we encounter situations that are impossible to balance without help.

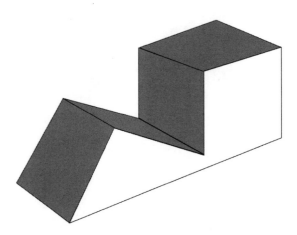

A belt can be useful for more than just holding up trousers. Draping a belt over the wooden object pictured above enables you to balance it on your finger. Amazing!

I think this works because the belt adds weight to the triangular part of the wooden shape. This weight makes a different force active upon the horizontally held finger.

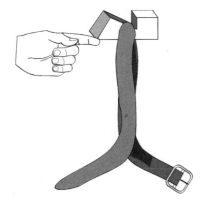

This is a simple trick, but it can be dressed up into an illustrative tale which suggests that just as the belt helps the wooden object to balance, the "belt of truth" (Eph. 6:14) can also help to balance many seemingly impossible life situations.

CHAPTER 8

The Language of the Heart

Communication has now been seriously studied in several areas of research. This shows a clear distinction between teaching well and learning well. We learn when a message becomes part of our experience. When our hearts are touched, the things we learn will be remembered.

Gaining more and more diplomas, degrees, and other professional qualifications may not always be helpful for spiritual growth. A Japanese pictogram combining the two characters for the words for DEAD and HEART are joined together to give the Japanese word for BUSY.

Words and explanations can actually be detrimental at times. Actions may indeed speak louder than words.

> The purpose of a fish trap is to catch fish, and when the fish are caught, the trap is forgotten. The purpose of a rabbit snare is to catch rabbits. When the rabbits are caught in the snare, the snare is forgotten. The purpose of words is to convey ideas. When the ideas are grasped, the words are forgotten. Where can I find a man who has forgotten words? He is the one I would like to talk to.[1]

> Words, even the agreed words, are only the beginning of worship. Those who use them do well to recognize their transience and imperfection; to treat them as a ladder, not a goal; to acknowledge their power in shaping faith and kindling devotion, without claiming that they are fully adequate to the task. Only the grace of God can make up for what is lacking in the faltering words of men.[2]

---

[1]A saying attributed to the Chinese philosopher Chang Tzu.
[2]Central Board of Finance of the Church of England, *Alternative Service Book* (1980), 11.

Two jesters were sent out into the world for a year by their king. Upon their return, the king summoned them and asked the first to draw a picture of the thing that had caused him the most happiness and blessing in the year he had been away. He requested that the second draw a picture of the thing that had caused him the most misery and pain. It was a great surprise to find both produced a drawing of the same thing: the tongue.[3]

The spears of the intellect guard the doors of the mind against the touching of the emotions. The attitude of the clown to people and situations will be as important as any skill he shows. This vulnerability will produce reactions — both *positively* in the release of spiritual gifts, and *negatively* in reactions of mockery, critical attitudes and even physical and verbal abuse. For this reason, it is wise to have clowns working together in pairs or small groups.

It is best not to hang around and argue with those who might want to disrupt the performance, even if you have a clever joke or way of handling the situation. This will show the difference between performance and ministry. When onlookers see you react in unexpected ways to new situations which develop, they will be powerfully affected. Do not defend or justify yourself, but do pray for the right actions or movements. Be guided by those with you. It is helpful to carry with you a bag full of "bits and pieces" (simple props, tricks, gifts, etc.) which can be used to deflect possible confrontation. Curiosity is a strong emotion. I recall on one occasion when some young teenagers were beginning to get out of hand, that one of the teens told the rest of them to be quiet because he wanted to see what was going to happen next. People love to see the clown produce surprises from a box or case.

Beware of becoming a clown in externals only. This can happen all too easily. Arthur "Vercoe" Pedlar,[4] writing about a dispute among clowns in the weeks leading up to the first

---

[3]James 3:1-12 expands on the double-edged nature of the tongue.

[4]Arthur Pedlar has been involved in clowning for over forty years, and began with the Cirque Medrano in Paris. He now teaches and lectures widely throughout the United Kingdom and beyond and continues to perform as well. He is a leading member of the World Clowns Association.

International Clown Summit in Scotland in 1989, put things extremely well when he wrote, " As soon as a clown stands on his dignity, it's time someone put a banana skin under him."[5]

A story is told about the Day of Atonement which expresses this more fully. It was the yearly custom in this place for the rabbi to enter the synagogue and put on sackcloth and ashes before the congregation.

He would then turn to the assembly and proclaim the prayer of humility which began, "I am but dust and ashes…"

One year the rabbi arrived earlier than usual at the synagogue to find the door slightly open. On further investigation, he saw the caretaker inside on his knees in prayer. "Nothing wrong with that," thought the rabbi, but he stood rooted to the spot when he heard the old man pray, "I am but dust and ashes…"

In a rage, the rabbi rushed into the synagogue and grabbed the poor man by the coat. "Who do you think you are to pray, 'I am but dust and ashes…'? *That's my job.*"

Floyd Shaffer pointed out that "Jesus promised his followers three things: that they would have joy, that others would think they were crazy and that they would have trouble." This illustrates how it is that the Christian minister, clown or not, is often perceived and received.

The questions of most significance in the examination of any ministry will center on the fruits of the Spirit,[6] e.g., "What is the harvest like?"

Of course this will seldom be easily measured, but my experience is that there is often a credibility gap between the claims and realities of Christian ministries. Many leaders stress the need for good Bible teaching and yet fail to see how little effect the teaching has actually had in changing attitudes and lives. Authentic, joyful living is a most powerful means of sharing the good news.

Many churches have been so afraid of emotionalism that they have allowed little room for the emotions. The clown helps

[5]In conversation at the time of the first International Clown Summit.
[6]Gal. 5:22-23.

to bring them back to their rightful place. He touches the emotions and brings forth a response, often laughter and/or tears.

One attractive tradition of the early church was to begin the Easter sermon with a joke. Death has lost its sting (1 Corinthians 15). Life that has lightness and laughter is a sign of health.

Laughter and Tears in Scripture

Few books have been written on the humor of Christ. It is difficult to find many places in the Gospels which are genuinely humorous to the Western mind, even when we are aware of the background and significance of the teaching. In the Old Testament, there are several words for laughter:

1) "To scoff" (Hebrew: *Laag*) at the unrighteous (Ps. 37:17); Job thinks "God laughs at the plight of the innocent" (Job 9:23).

2) "To laugh along with" (Hebrew: *Tsechoq*) (Gen. 21:6).

3) "To laugh at a joke" (Hebrew: *Teshaq*). In the wonderful story of the birth of Isaac, his given name is linked with laughter (Gen. 17:17). This puts humor into the center of the Jewish trinity of Abraham, Isaac, and Jacob. It is more like a snicker than tinkling laughter — laughing *at* God rather than enjoying his promises.

4) "To laugh in the face of danger," "to dismiss as unimportant" (Hebrew: *Sachaq*). God laughs at the whirring javelin (Job 41:29). The virtuous will laugh at the fate of the evil man (Ps. 52:6).

The Orthodox church teaches that holy laughter is a spiritual gift from God. Holy laughter is gentle, light, releasing, controlled and full of happiness. It has been compared to a bubbling brook. There are many such examples of this kind of "joy in the Lord." It includes the full health and strength of the faithful life. It is particularly remembered in the autumn festival of the Jewish nation celebrated as the Feast of Tabernacles. This joy can overflow into healing laughter. One of the early church fathers said, "I met the devil, he was serious. I met God, he laughed and danced." Jesus' teaching centers on joy (John 16:22).

J. C. McLelland asks the question, "Is life worth celebrating in spite of its contradictions?" His answer is a definite "Yes."

> The art of clowning is the humane art in which man finds his way to the center, the definite place at which God promises to meet him. It taps resources of which tragedy, for all its insight and its nobility, is ignorant. Knowing he is a fool, the clown chooses to act the part, and so discovers a pattern of truth. If he responds to that pattern and opens his life to the power of the clown with passion, it is called *faith*. If through laughter he serves his fellows and shares their lot, it is called *love*. If he moves towards God as the joy of present and future, it is called *hope*. So faith, hope and love affirm the pattern and commend it to others. The jesting spirit has been loosed among us. Who can resist it?[7]

"In the evening, sadness, but in the morning, gladness."[8]

Tears are more commonly evidenced in Scripture than laughter, though this again is not always quite what it might seem. Crying isn't always a sign of sadness, but it does signify a response of the emotions to events and circumstances. Again, the Eastern Orthodox church teaches about this:

> There are two kinds of breaking: one gentle and the other to glory.
>
> There is a breaking of the heart which is gentle and makes it deeply penitent, and there is a breaking of the heart that is violent and harmful, shattering it completely.[9]
>
> Initial joy is one thing, the joy of perfection another. The first is not exempt from fantasy, while the second has the strength of humility. Between the

---

[7]J. C. McLelland, *The Clown and the Crocodile* (Atlanta: John Knox Press, 1968), 119 (Italics mine).

[8]Ps. 30:5, author's paraphrase.

[9]Quotation of St. Mark the Hermit. St. Makarios of Athos and St. Makarios of Corinth, comps., *The Philokalia* (Venice, 1782). I used the version published by Faber & Faber (London) in 1979 (vol. 1, page 111).

two comes a godly sorrow (I Corinthians 7:10) and active tears (that is, tears unaccompanied by grief).[10]

In our society, tears are not encouraged. Such is the fear of emotionalism, that any show of individual emotion is discouraged. The saying "Laugh, and the world laughs with you; cry, and you cry alone" has become, "Look and see if the world is laughing or crying and do the same. Then you will not stand out as different." Some parents scold their children for crying in public, even if they hurt themselves badly. Crying is seen to be weak and unacceptable. Yet tears can flow for all sorts of reasons, such as grief, emotional relief, rage and joy.

This is the journey that the Christian clown encourages all to take: from intitial joy through the breaking and hurtful experiences of life, to a deeper joy which is centered on a new kingdom.

---

[10]Quotation of St. Mark the Hermit. St. Makarios of Athos and St. Makarios of Corinth, comps., *The Philokalia* (Venice, 1782). I used the version published by Faber & Faber (London) in 1979 (vol. 1, page 271).

PAPER CROSS

(Use paper that is colored on one side only, such as origami paper.)

- - - - means VALLEY FOLD   - - - means MOUNTAIN FOLD

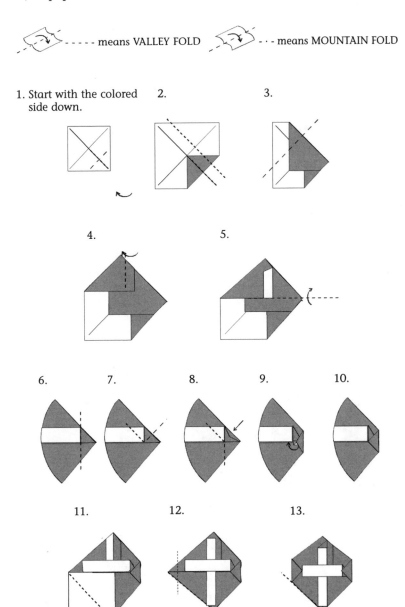

1. Start with the colored side down.
2.
3.
4.
5.
6.
7.
8.
9.
10.
11.
12.
13.

CHAPTER 9

It's Not What You Do, It's the Way That You Do It

When I was a teenager, I once sent too much money for an order to a supplier of magical goods. In return, he included a little booklet (which has since gone out of print) by the stage performer Edward Maurice. The booklet gave details of theatrical makeup and deportment; however, the title was as good as the whole book for me. It was called, *Showmanship and Presentation* with the subtitle *No Tricks — Only the Things That Matter.*[1]

The clown as minister doesn't act the clown, any more than the preacher acts the preacher. There needs to be an "inner consistency" that directly relates to everyday life and behavior. Each of us must be the clown (child) God calls us to be. Randall Bane is an American performing artist who is well known for the integrity of his performance. He was a dancer and later a director of Christian festivals. He is currently involved in the annual presentation in Jerusalem of the Feast of Tabernacles planned by the Christian Embassy. When he first became a Christian, Randall, who had been trained in the theatre, wanted to use his gifts for Christian outreach. This led him to develop a clown character whom he called O-Bie Good. He began to feel that the clown character was too limiting, so he developed movement to music while still using the classic white face. My first encounter with Randall was over ten years ago, and I was impressed by his faithful dependence on the Lord. The gift he exercises is consistent with his lifestyle and spiritual understanding. His testimony to God's love for his creation is therefore especially winsome.

---

[1]Edward Maurice, *Showmanship and Presentation* (Birmingham, England: Goodliffe Publications, 1946).

Former monk Paul Baker is another performing artist who has helped me in my understanding of ministry. While Paul would not call himself a clown, his life story contains much encouragement to others interested in holy folly. In his first book,[2] Paul tells of how one simple decision to create a musical instrument out of an old drawer completely changed his life.

> Father Aloysius's drawer came as a complete revelation. After all, a delicately shaped guitar bears little obvious relation to a square, blunt drawer broken on one side and half-submerged in a flood of just-cleared-out rubbish, yet in that drawer the solution to my difficulties lay open and obvious: make one. I hadn't the least idea how to set about the task, but by using the drawer as a base, perhaps it would be possible to work out the fundamental principles. So surreptitious happenings began in the carpenter's shop. It was overlooked by the novitiate and the students' room, so I stole in after dark or before dawn, always choosing moments when everyone else was likely to be engaged in reading or meditation or some other stationary and consuming occupation. A month or so later, having broken just about every known law of guitar construction, I begged some string from the family and set one on. The sound was...good![3]

The making of the guitar was a key event in Paul's decision to move out of the monastery. As he put it, "The tiny, tiny step of making the guitar rather than buying one contained the germ of the whole of the marvelous life to follow, in hidden expectancy."[4] He has become involved in the needs of the Third World, traveling and singing songs to the accompaniment of his guitar all over the world.

The clown is allowed to have fun and to help others see behind the labels and categories that are given and received too

---

[2]Baker, Paul, *Of Minstrels, Monks and Milkmen* (London: S.C.M., 1981).
[3]Ibid., 111.
[4]Ibid., 163.

readily. The clown is never daunted by what others might deem to be impossible. He will always try, and in the very trying can never be a failure.

There is a wonderful scene in the David Lean film *Lawrence of Arabia*, when one of the members of Lawrence's party is left behind in the desert. He asks the others whether or not they should go back. His companions tell him that this would mean certain death, and that fate will decide what will happen. "It is written," they said. Lawrence does not accept this and turns his camel back into the desert. He does find the missing man and rescues him. This earned him a new title among the Arabs — "The man for whom it is *not* written."

What better description could there be for the Christian clown? "The one for whom it is *not* written." The Christian clown is not willing to work under the constraints of negative thought. He is always ready to step out in faith.

The clown turns things upside down, or depending on your perspective, right side up. This is a way of viewing the world which is totally consistent, if you accept the possibility of living in a different way. It is not accurate to say that Christian clowning is "based on a violation of the logical and the use of the extreme," as experienced clown teacher and author Jack Wiley proposes.[5] The clown is not illogical — rather, he pursues a line of reason which differs markedly from the cultural norm. The former Anglican bishop of Singapore, the Right Reverend Ban It Chiu, was trained as a lawyer in London before his ordination. He once told me of how he used to delight in using story and analogy in his legal submissions. This greatly disturbed those who claimed a logical approach was the "right" way to argue a case, and he was accused of being illogical. He pointed out that such a view was not universal. He also remarked that for all their logical approach, most lawyers he knew constantly used storytelling techniques.

---

[5]Jack Wiley, *Basic Circus, Juggling, Unicycling, Bicycling and Clowning Skills* (n.p.: Solipaz Publishing Co., 1983), 198.

The following story was used a few years ago by a trial lawyer trying to convince a jury not to bring in a guilty verdict on his client.

Once there was a smart kid who longed to get the better of a wise old man. No matter what the boy asked, the wise man could always come up with the right answer. Determined to get the better of him, the kid came up with a plan. He went into the forest and caught a small bird. He cupped it in his hands and carried it to the wise man. He planned to ask the man, "Is what I have in my hands alive or dead?"

If the man said "Dead," then he would simply release the bird, but should the man say "Alive," then he would squeeze his hands together and kill the bird. This time he was certain he would outsmart the wise man. As he drew close, he asked, "Is the thing I am holding alive or dead?"

The old man paused, looked straight into the young man's eyes and said, "The answer lies in your hands."

Often questions and answers unlock a whole new level of understanding. They may open up a totally new way of thinking.

A tourist visiting one of the Pacific islands observed a man and his son rod-fishing from a river bank. They had one large fish lying beside them, had just pulled out a second and then set out for home.

"Excuse me," said the tourist, "but why don't you get a second rod for your son?"

"Why?" asked the man.

"Then you could catch more fish."

"Why should we catch more?" asked the man again.

"You could buy a net and catch even more, and then sell them in the market."

"Why would we do that?"

"Well, then you could buy a boat, and eventually a whole fleet of boats, and become very rich," continued the visitor.

The fisherman frowned, puzzled at this suggestion. Finally he asked, "Why should I want to do that?"

"Why, then you could take an afternoon off any time you liked and *go fishing with your son.*"

Extreme behavior is not a necessity of clown-type behavior. Some clowns are far more effective when underwhelming their audience rather than overwhelming them with zany and way-out skills. Those starting out in clowning usually begin with brightly colored costumes and startling makeup. This often changes as the clown gains more experience. I find the clowns that have had the most profound effect on me have a naturalistic appearance. Their makeup is lightly applied with perhaps only one or two features marked in brown or red. Their costumes tend to be just a little bit unusual and not extreme in size or color. This is not to dismiss other approaches, but it has been my experience that clowns are far more approachable and winsome in simple outfits.

In a church that was new to clown ministry, the following sketch was developed. At the beginning of the service, one man, dressed smartly in a suit, entered and knelt down in front of the altar and began to pray. A clown came in by the back door, blowing soap bubbles and wandering toward the front of the church. He was seemingly oblivious to the congregation. As he neared the front, the first man noticed the clown for the first time and in a loud whisper demanded, "What are you doing here? Don't you know we are going to have a service? Please *go away.*"

The clown (remember that the clown I am most interested in is the one who does not intrude where he is not welcome) turned to leave. Just then, someone in the congregation (who had been previously prepared) stood up and read aloud, "The foolishness of God is wiser than the wisdom of man."[6]

Grudgingly, the first man allowed the clown to stay, but insisted that he did nothing to interrupt or distract the wor-

[6]1 Cor. 1:25, author's paraphrase.

shipers. The clown was very grateful and again turned to sit down, but then as an afterthought offered his bubble mixture to the man, so that he would also blow a bubble. The smart gentleman was shocked at the idea and held up his hands in horror. Then the reader read out a second passage: "Unless you become like a child, you cannot enter the kingdom of heaven."[7]

Hesitantly, he began to blow some bubbles, and his enjoyment increased with each bubble.

That was the end of the sketch, but on one occasion a large bubble continued to float upwards, on the warm air currents, toward the roof of the church. The numerous large windows and light sources filled the bubble with sparkling rainbow color. Everything stopped for a full minute as we waited to see what would happen.

This moment of waiting was extremely full. The clown had called a halt to things in order that everyone could enjoy the passing joy of a soap bubble. Foolish, yet wonderful.

Ken Feit tells of one sunny day when he was a student. He had been reading outside. Because he had been engrossed in his book and sitting very still, amazingly, a spider had begun to weave a web between his left-hand thumb and finger. Ken says he was faced with a dilemma: whether to stay still to allow the spider to finish or go to his next lecture. This would only be a question a genuine fool would struggle with, yet it does show a heart concern for the foolish and weak things of God's creation.

When Dr. Albert Schweitzer, a well-known medical missionary to Africa, was building his first hospital at Lambarere, the locals remembered his concern for even the smallest parts of creation. After the holes had been dug for the hospital building, Albert would reach down into each one and lift out any insect that might have fallen in, so that it would not be crushed when the pole was put in place.

A sketch I use on occasion which relates to this begins with the clown carrying in a large box which is labeled "clown costume." When he opens the first box, he finds another smaller

[7]Matt. 18:3, author's paraphrase.

box inside. On opening this, yet another smaller box is inside, and so on until only a tiny box remains. Carefully opening this, the clown gently removes a small heart made out of red felt. He puts this little heart into a special shirt pocket, which is just above his heart. The point is that the only costume a clown needs is the right kind of heart.

I have, through my interest in origami, a fine range of models and shapes that I can make from a sheet of newspaper. After some practice, I wrote a poem on the story of Jonah ("Jonah," page 133).

It begins with Jonah looking at the local paper to find a ship on which he might escape from God's command to go to Nineveh. The paper folds into a boat, then into a captain's hat, a whale's mouth, and so on. Paper is used to make a giant tree for Jonah to sit under and find shade, and also for a row of men and cattle that God cares about too much to destroy. By the end, the floor is usually strewn with folded, torn or shredded paper.

The first time I performed this, I realized, as I was nearing the finish, that it would be good to "clean up my own mess." This was a long time before I had ever heard of Fulghum and his book.[8] So when the sketch was over and applauded, I went off and got a broom and dustpan and spent the next few minutes tidying up every last scrap of paper from the floor. Afterward, I found out that it was this act of tidying up, just as much as the clever use of paper shapes, that spoke to the audience. I had not planned to do this, but now I am always careful to tidy up all the mess I make. It has a profound effect on the caretakers and janitors of the properties and saves them a little bit of work in the process, since I have swept at least some of the floor for them.

The characteristics of spiritual inner consistency and individuality in clowns who serve God, may be summed up in a traditional Jewish story concerning David's harp.

Young David, a shepherd boy, was brought to the court of

[8]Robert Fulghum, *All I Really Needed to Know I Learned in Kindergarten: Uncommon Thoughts on Common Things* (New York: Villard Books, 1988).

King Saul, and soon became everybody's favorite. Once, when the court was assembled, he asked the King's permission to play a harp which was lying near the King's throne.

The King replied, "I have been deceived by the one who made it. Nobody could ever play on it. It only produces discord."

David insisted. When he touched the strings of the harp with his fingers, the instrument began to rejoice and weep at his command. The music was so glorious that when he finished, everyone was in tears.

The King asked him, "How is it that all the others could not play this harp and you could?"

David answered, "All the others tried to play their own song. I reminded her of the beautiful times when she was a young tree in the forest, when birds chirped in her branches, and when her leaves were bathed in sunlight and you heard the joy of the harp. Then I told her of my sympathy for the suffering through which she passed on the terrible day when men cut down the tree. But its death had not been in vain. For out of its wood, a harp was made on which God's praises could be played. And the harp rejoiced when she understood her calling."

When the Messiah comes, many will try to play their own songs on his harp. The result will be a religion of terrible ugliness. But there will always be the chosen ones who will play his songs — the songs of eternal glory, of humbling sorrow, death and new life. Tune your instruments for playing his song.[9]

---

[9]Another version of this story about David's harp may be found in Mary O'Hara, *A Celebration of Love* (London: Hodder and Stoughton, 1985), 63.

THE BUTTERFLY STORY

A simple story board may be constructed for many tales. Work out the main incidents, and remember that each stage will need to be related to the previous one. I have used this technique for telling the stories of "Truth and Parable" (page 7), and "The Juggler of God" (page 63). Work out the ideas with paper flaps, then tape the card together for the final form. Make sure you learn the order in which the flaps are to be turned over.

1.

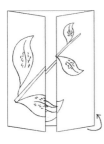

Small black eggs on the underside of the leaves...

2.

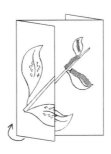

...hatch into caterpillars.

3.

The caterpillars grow bigger, eating up the leaves...

4.

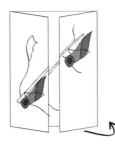

...and then turn into pupae.

5.

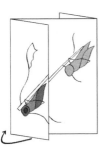

After a few weeks, the pupae open...

6.

...and the butterflies emerge.

CHAPTER 10

Clown Skills

Relationships and proper preparation are vitally important in Christian clowning. We have noted again and again the way that the clown is seldom the intrusive character of the popular image of fun-maker, but far more the one who draws others into his own world. This world is full of new possibilities and hope for those who are trapped or imprisoned by negative and critical attitudes.

These inner qualities are real skills to be learned and developed, but they do not excuse us from putting in the practice needed to learn more traditional clown skills. Each clown will find one skill or another to be more suited to his or her abilities and interests. Roly Bain,[1] an Anglican clergyman, became one of the first full-time Christian clowns in England. He tells of how, during his training at Fool Time, a clown college in Bristol, he found many of the skills very difficult, but discovered that he greatly enjoyed walking the slack rope. (This is like a tightrope but slack.) He now travels with this as a main part of his performance as an acted parable of faith.

The skills we choose to work on will depend on our temperament, natural ability and, perhaps most of all, on our perseverance. The latter is essential. It may also be that working on a particular skill may become obsessive, so it is important to keep a sense of proportion and a sense of humor.

In learning any skill, it is important to keep in mind exactly how the skill might be used. Even the process of learning might in itself be used as a clown sketch. I have a piece called "The Juggling Lesson" (page 168), in which a tape teaches the clown to juggle. It begins simply, but ends up with the tape voice "responding" to the mistakes and blunders and, eventually to the clown's success. It is based on a real juggling lesson. The

[1]Roly Bain has recently written *Fools Rush In* (London: Marshall & Pickering, 1993).

illusion was so complete that one child asked if she could borrow the tape for her father because he would like to juggle but had never been able to yet. If you pretend to learn a skill as part of your act, remember to caution against drawing too much attention to your actual skill, thus distracting from the message you are trying to convey.

There are, of course, certain times when the clown deliberately draws attention to himself. Yet this should be as an act of service rather than of self-glorification. In rodeos, clowns are used as a distraction for the crowd or the animals in the event of anything going wrong. This requires great courage and involves taking risks. Any fear or tension is lessened by the presence of clowns.

A farmer friend of mine tells me that if he has a field of cows that are a bit skittish, he puts a donkey in the field with them. This always has a calming effect on the cows, and the donkey does nothing but eat grass. I find this similar to the role of the clown.

The song "Send in the Clowns" tells the story of a circus disaster. It is about a trapeze artist duo. The woman, "late in her career," has fallen. She looks up from the ground to see her partner dangling in midair. Yet the show must go on, so she sings "Send in the clowns. There's got to be clowns..." Clowns are not permitted the luxury of natural reaction to tragedy. Their role in such a situation is to serve others and prevent panic.

When he was a young man, Kasahara, one of Japan's leading paper-folders, was troubled by some criticism of his art form. He began to wonder if folding paper was a worthwhile way to spend a life. He shares movingly how he was reassured when, soon after this, he taught a terminally ill young boy to fold birds and animals out of colored paper. It seemed to him an eminently worthwhile way of life.

Author Heidi Britz[2] from Germany, whose specialty is storytelling and related subjects told me the following story:

---

[2]Heidi Britz, *Children at Play: A Preparation for Life* (Edinburgh: Floris Books, 1972).

Heidi Britz — Storyteller

I met a mother of four children whom I had not seen for some years. She told me that her eldest daughter was not able to learn to read or write, so they sent her to the "small class" (similar to a special education class in the United States) of Stuttgart Waldorf School. There, they taught those children — all with learning difficulties — to ride a unicycle and juggle at the same time using three rings or three clubs. The children felt grand and had lots of fun with this — and without special training, they learned to read and write quite suddenly, just by acquiring the ability to concentrate on what they were doing. At our St. John's Fire Festival, that girl, Berenike, was juggling with three fire torches.

There is positive value in skill-teaching, even when such clear and encouraging responses are not immediately forthcoming. The very process of freely sharing a skill is in itself liberating.

It might be an obvious thing to say, but it is best to begin with skills you already have and to add to these little by little.

For example, if you play a musical instrument, think of ways you might be able to use music in your performance. Even if you can only play one tune well, you may be able to build a whole sketch around it.

Or it may be that you have some acrobatic or balancing skill. Don't feel anything is too simple. One of the most impressive clown acts I have seen lasted about fifteen minutes and consisted of the clown trying various ways of balancing on a stool. The final balance was a handstand on the top of the stool to thunderous applause.

If you can balance a broom handle on the palm of your hand, you will be able to balance other things quite successfully. Look for objects that are top-heavy, as they balance best. Try using a peacock tail feather. This creates a very pleasing effect and is quite easy to balance on the top of your nose.

Always be ready to pick up new ideas. It is useful to keep a notebook of anything you see or hear that appeals to you. I find the early Hollywood movies often have incredibly clever little pieces in them that are not well-known. They may take some practice, but often are well worth the effort. New ideas may also be picked up at clown and mime courses.

Very little of the material clowns use is totally original. The skill lies in the routining or putting together ideas and "bits of business." The final presentation should flow and appear to be logical and natural, though it may take a long time to get to this point.

Development of Clown Sketches

The process of development of a clown sketch may go something like this:

1) **Basic Idea.** Observing another performer, seeing a particular skill in action or hearing a joke that suggests itself for possible adaptation to a visual medium.

2) **Experiment With the Basic Idea.** Practicing the skills involved and adding beginning and ending material. Presenting the material to a sympathetic yet critical audience.

3) **Develop the Sketch as a Piece on Its Own.** This is the end of the road for most performers, but for the clown there is yet one more step.

4) **Practice.** Run through the sketch numerous times so that any skills in the sketch appear to be so simple that anyone could do them, though the final effect will show that this is not so. There is something very attractive about a clown who seems to be clumsy and unable to do simple tasks such as tying his shoelaces, and yet rides a unicycle with ease.

There are currently many props and clown materials available. Even so, I find it well worthwhile, when possible, to make my own equipment. This gives a freedom to experiment and also to develop specific items to suit your particular needs. Another great advantage is that should something break, then it is possible to make another without reordering from a distant source. It is not uncommon for things to disappear from a clown during and after a performance. If you make your own equipment, the loss does not present such a great problem, and it may offer an opportunity to remake and redesign the prop. This also helps keep clowns happily foolish about such things. Do not carry anything irreplaceable with you if you are performing on your own in a public setting. It will be almost impossible to relate fully to the audience if you are keeping an eye on your case at the same time. It is usually best to carry all you need on your person, in pockets or bags. This again creates a special interest. The clown becomes a traveling treasure box of surprises.

I recently found a quilt at a sale which has a large, silk-screened picture of a clown on it. I carefully cut slits in the pockets of the clown's costume and sewed real pockets behind them. This will be used as a backdrop in one sketch, where this "clown assistant" will from time to time supply juggling balls, handkerchiefs and strings to the performer. Each new prop will come from a different pocket and will give the illusion of a two-dimensional object becoming three-dimensional.

Philip Noble juggling homemade clubs.

A good set of juggling clubs can be made from a set of children's plastic bowling pins by cutting off the tops and lengthening the clubs to about twenty inches with a piece of broom handle. Refix the top knob on the other end of the wooden insert. This should be glued and nailed in place. Wind the wooden handle with strips of toweling and secure everything with colored tape. Since the bowling pins come in sets of ten, spare sets of clubs may be made for teaching purposes.

There are, of course, some props that require the knowledge of a specialist. It is well worth it to ask for help from local craftsmen as well as to check with clown supply outlets. A few years ago, Roly Bain got some new clown shoes. They had been specially made for him by a local shoemaker and, while quite expensive, they were of the highest quality and made to his specific design. The cover of Roly's book has an excellent photograph of Roly on the slack wire. He is wearing these same shoes, and they still look as good as new.[3] As I mentioned earlier, my clown costume and wig were made for me by friends, and for the story "Truth and Parable" (page 7). I asked an acquaintance who is a skilled cartoonist to make large drawings of the characters which I pasted onto boards (see page 83). In the telling of the story, I use these pictures to illustrate the tale.

One of the benefits of learning new skills is that you have the opportunity to share your newfound information with others by teaching at a workshop. Many people are becoming interested in circus and clown skills, and even the basic techniques of juggling and clown makeup are not yet widely known. This gives a good opportunity to share insights that have been gained during hours of practice. Basic skills can be taught quite quickly to most groups, and then time is given for individuals to develop at their own rate. I now teach juggling at the end of workshops — one reason being that those who are not interested can drift away easily, and another being that if the group is young and high-spirited, there is the possibility that the juggling balls might be used as missiles! It is much easier to control this at the end of a session. Those who are beginning to make progress can stay a little longer for more practice. I do not usually try to teach three-ball juggling to beginners at the first session. I will instead try to teach all the possible tricks and patterns that can be done with one ball, such as throwing and catching with different hands behind the back; clapping, jumping, and tumbling while throwing and catching the ball; or working out simple routines in twos and threes with one ball each. This means everyone can achieve at least some success quickly and gain practice in throwing and catching the balls.

Trick Roping

When I was about twelve years old, I bought a rope designed

---

[3]Bain, *Fools Rush In.*

for trick roping, rope spinning, as it is called in the United Kingdom. After many attempts, I gave up trying to make it work properly. Then some twenty years later, a rope spinner called Vince Bruce appeared on a TV variety show. Vince, who calls himself the "Cockney Cowboy," reawakened my interest with some amazing jumps, loop twirls and catches. Through the producer of the program, I managed to make contact with him, and he has been kind enough to give me a great deal of help and advice over the years. I managed to make the basic loops fairly quickly, but still hope to become even more proficient. I have never had any direct contact with a trick roper, and though there are some excellent books on the subject,[4] I have found it even harder to learn than juggling.

Trick roping is a high-energy activity and requires a large space. It is also worth checking if the costume that you wear is suitable. I once lost my clown wig with a final fling of the rope. Now I only include trick roping in a program when I am not in full clown costume.

Bubble Liquid

For some years now, I have been looking for a mixture that would produce good, long-lasting soap bubbles. I began with kitchen experiments using everything that I thought might possibly work, including shampoos, car wash liquid and soaps of all sorts. I even tried making my own soap, which I do not recommend, as it proved to be an extremely smelly process.

My next step was to consult my local pharmacy, and this was the beginning of an exciting journey. While the pharmacist could not help, he did supply the information that my quest actually dealt with, a branch of physical chemistry. So I went right to the top and wrote to the Professor of Physical Chemistry at Glasgow University, asking for advice. He put me in touch with his colleague in Edinburgh, who supplied a full and precise recipe. Wonderful, except that most of the chemicals could not be obtained in small quantities or across the counter in any shop.

[4]Frank Dean, *Will Rogers' Rope Tricks* (Colorado Springs, Colorado: Western Horseman Publications, 1969).

Fortunately, I had friends who had contacts in the chemistry field. I was able to obtain all of the substances except one, sodium algenate. Then one day I learned that there was only one factory in the United Kingdom that produced this, and it was within easy reach of our home. I also learned that sodium algenate was actually seaweed! A visit to the factory produced a very positive response from a man in a white coat who, upon learning of the reason for my interest, kindly supplied me with two small bags of sodium algenate — one of fine grains and the other of coarser grains. Making up the mixture proved quite arduous, but it did give excellent bubbles. I managed to keep one in a jar (free from air currents) for over three days. I later found out that the record life of a soap bubble is over 300 days, so there is room for improvement in my bubble mixture development.

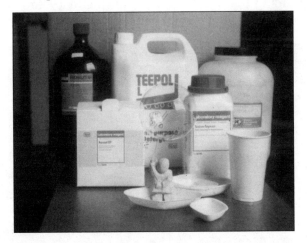

Ingredients for soap bubbles

Many of my friends became interested in my quest, and my mother, during a visit to the United States, came across some bubble liquid and a marvelous bubble trumpet.[5] This contact opened many new doors, and also led me to David Stein's Bubble Thing.[6] This wonderful device was developed by David

[5]Available from Tangent Toy Company, Box 436, 10 Liberty Ship Way, Suite 147, Sausalito, CA 94965.
[6]J. Cassidy & D. Stein, *The Unbelievable Bubble Book* (Palo Alto: Klutz Publications, 1987). Stein's Bubble Thing is attached to this book.

as he was seeking to make larger and larger frames with which to form larger and larger soap bubbles. He made the discovery that if he formed a flexible frame, it could be folded and dipped into bubble liquid. Huge bubbles could be produced with a much smaller quantity of bubble mixture than was previously required.

He eventually simplified this idea into a straight plastic stick with a loop of soft, absorbent material attached at one point on the far end with another point on the loop of material fixed to a sliding handle on the plastic stick.

To make a large bubble, the closed fabric loop is dipped into a small tub of bubble liquid and then, as the stick is withdrawn, the handle slides the loop open to give a large soap film. By waving the stick gently sideways and then closing off the loop by sliding the handle to close off the loop, large bubbles may be made.

Bubble Thing in action

It was at this time that I came across a very simple and effective bubble liquid which could be quickly made. The ingredients are glycerine, Dawn or Joy dishwashing liquid and water, roughly in the proportion 1:2:10. Unfortunately, Dawn and Joy dishwashing liquids aren't readily available in the United Kingdom at present, and the manufacturers were unable to suggest equivalent products when asked. Fortunately, friends and relatives always bring back a bottle or two for me when they travel, and now a few shops are beginning to supply liquids especially for making large bubbles.

Here is a word of caution for anyone trying to make large soap bubbles: They are very temperamental. In particular, they are easily affected by air currents, too much carbon dioxide, too little humidity, and by small children who just love to burst them. One way of handling the latter is to make an agreement allowing the children to burst some bubbles at the beginning and end of the performance if they will allow you to set some free in between. This sometimes works.

A final word of advice: If you are working with large quantities of bubble liquid inside, cover the floor with a cloth that can be washed later. Never try to clean up spilled bubble liquid using a mop and water, as this simply produces masses of bubbles. This might be the basis of a clown sketch, but remember that it will have to be tidied up by somebody later. To clean up most effectively, use dry paper towels.

A presentation using soap bubbles is particularly effective when accompanied by music or sound effects. It is worth seeking help with this as once the tape is made, it can be used again and again.

BUBBLE IN A BUBBLE

1) Blow a medium-sized bubble, and then soak a straw in bubble liquid. Gently push the straw into the bubble and blow.

2) A small stream of bubbles will spin into the bubble and drift toward the bottom.

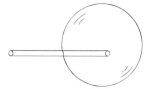

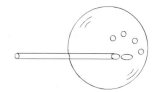

3) The small bubbles will tend to fall to the bottom of the big bubble and join the bubble skin, but if you keep the bubble afloat, at least one or two should survive.

Another somewhat harder way of doing this is to blow a fairly large bubble, and then blow the side so that it collapses inwards. When this works, it is very beautiful.

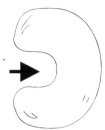

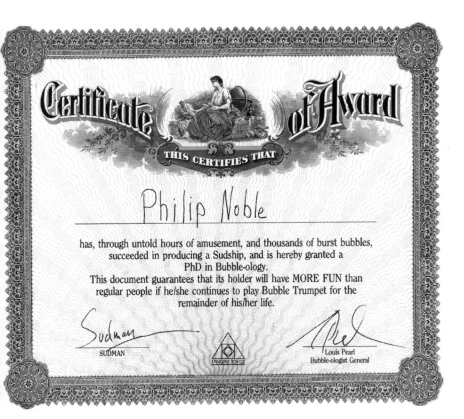

Certificate of Award

THIS CERTIFIES THAT

Philip Noble

has, through untold hours of amusement, and thousands of burst bubbles, succeeded in producing a Sudship, and is hereby granted a PhD in Bubble-ology.

This document guarantees that its holder will have MORE FUN than regular people if he/she continues to play Bubble Trumpet for the remainder of his/her life.

SUDMAN

TANGENT TOY CO

Louis Pearl
Bubble-ologist General

CHAPTER 11
Clown Ideas

Most people starting out in clown ministry find it very hard to develop new material and struggle with this in the early days. Remember that very little clown material is totally original, and that adapting and reworking familiar themes forms the basis for most of the clown's resources. However, as the material is used and performers "make it their own," changes and developments take place, often almost imperceptibly. I recently reread a story I tell often in its original source book. I was amazed to see how it differed from the story I tell. While the main theme was recognizable, I had lengthened some parts, added an introduction and changed some of the details. I regard this as a good sign.

Initially, books of sketches are helpful in the preparation of material. These will need to be audience tested and often require much adaptation to suit specific clowns and their own circumstances.

Let me reemphasize that it is wise to keep a notebook of ideas and sketches that might be useful in the future. I now have about six notebooks full of all sorts of ideas and visual effects that I have encountered over the years. When developing a new sketch, I will often flip through their pages and discover something that generates a new twist or an improvement at one point or another. In these notebooks, I jot down *anything* that might be of use: stories, comments overheard on a bus, simple diagrams, logos, puzzles, riddles or whatever else comes my way. Children are a great source of new material. To give an example, I recently discovered that SILENT is an anagram for LISTEN. This led me to write the following short poem:

S - I - L - E - N - T

Parting the golden letters,
The storyteller paused,

The audience hushed.
He began to stitch
A tale together.

L - I - S - T - E - N

This poem could be developed into a clown sketch. Six helpers, each carrying or wearing one of the letters S, I, L, E, N, T, could arrange and rearrange themselves in different ways until the main performer or storyteller arrives. The final arrangement of the word "listen" could be followed by the clowns quietly and slowly taking their places to encourage an attentive audience.

This applies to other occasions also. There is a wonderful gift in being able to be still and truly listen to others, whether performers or preachers. This gift of concentration can be culti-vated. It makes for authentic clown relationships. The difficulty of most performances is that the individual has to be "good," and this brings with it the possibility of competition and rivalry. The clown should always leave others feeling better about them-selves and their situations, even if this is costly in time or materials. Jean Vanier writes of the importance of paying atten-tion at meetings as a sign of respect for others, even though we may not agree with them or find them interesting.[1]

An important part of the "lowly nature" of the clown is to value others above himself. The quality of attention we bring to our everyday encounters and meetings is extremely significant. Others notice how we react to those who are "less attractive," and the courtesy and patience with which we listen to people who may be nervous or insecure are the best indicators of the quality of our participation.

New products are being discovered and brought out every year. There are some that are "rediscovered" traditional ones, but occasionally there are some real innovations. They can be very useful in clowning, as they will make an immediate contact with the audience. What a nice surprise when the phone

---

[1] Jean Vanier, *Community and Growth* (London: D.L.T., 1979), 213.

is put on hold to find the standard tune played is a well-known hymn. Rather than becoming frustrated with this, perhaps the clown today would begin the conversation with a snatch of song in response. What about a conversation between answering machines? Two clowns pretending to be answering machines could begin to make their own arrangements, reverting to "machines" as soon as their privacy is invaded.

The Rubik's Cube

I first saw the Rubik's Cube in 1979 in the back of a Renault van in Paris. It was the last evening of a conference on play and Emile Kamenov, Yugoslavian Professor of Play, showed it to me. It was so amazing and unusual that I was more intrigued by the construction than by trying to solve the puzzle itself. How could twenty-seven small cubes be fixed together and yet move independently? It took me three days of intense thought before I hit on a way in which this could be constructed. It was not the way that Professor Rubik uses, but it gave me great satisfaction.

I have used the Rubik's Cube in several ways:

1) The clown can solve it extremely quickly by peeling off the little colored squares and rearranging them. (This needs some preparation with sticky colored paper squares that will adhere again after they are peeled off.)

2) A clown sketch for three clowns which we used, called *Mighty Marvo and Mini Marvo,* consisted of a magician, his trainee assistant and a presenter. The great magician gets all the tricks wrong, while his assistant succeeds every time, much to the frustration of the star. The final part was a demonstration of solving the Rubik's Cube within the world record of thirty seconds. Again, the assistant triumphs while the "expert" fails. This is how it worked. Two Rubik's Cubes are lying on the table, ready for the finale. The clown assistant innocently turns the tray around when he brings it forward, and so the magician gets the "wrong" one. After about twenty seconds, the helper simply lifts up the other Cube and steps forward. With one move, he solves the Cube. The one he has picked up is a com-

pleted Cube that has been covered with a loose-fitting shell (fived-sided cube) and decorated with the little colored squares peeled from a spare Cube. Thus, the proud are humbled and the humble exalted.

3) Rubik's Cubes come in different shapes, from barrels to spheres. They are of a nice size and weight to juggle.

4) A completely blank cube can have a very therapeutic effect, and everyone can enjoy it without having to worry about solving the puzzle.

Other toys or objects that might be useful for clown sketches are yo-yos, balloons, feather dusters and silk scarves.

Some jokes or puns can be turned into clown sketches very readily. They will speak of God's love and wit. In general, it is better to leave the theological application of any sketch to the preacher or leader of a meeting. The clowns are, as Barnum is often quoted as saying, "the pegs on which to hang the circus." The Christian clowns are the awakeners and enablers who draw attention to the fact that God is alive and real.

To begin creating new sketches for yourself and others, it may be helpful to consider words or ideas that are opposites, i.e., light-dark, strong-weak, adult-child, wise-foolish and proud-humble. Many of the Psalms and Proverbs center on such themes. They can be fruitful source material.

It is useful to carry with you some things to give away to people as signs of friendship. It is even better if you can make some things simply, such as balloon animals or paper-folded birds. Simple skills can then be taught as well, and this, too, can be a valuable present. The recipient can then pass on the free gift to others. This applies to the teaching of the skill also, as the most important gift you can give is the gift of attention. The very act of giving away has a real healing power in our self-centered world. This is even more true in the giving away of time.[2]

Whatever the material we develop, it will be most effective when it overflows from our everyday Christian life. Unless our

---

[2]Time, it is said, is a versatile performer. It flies, marches on, heals all wounds, runs out, will tell, and waits for no man.

performance is an expression of normal Christian life, it will not stand the close scrutiny of those we seek to relate to. We must beware of becoming people who deal in unlived truths. As Ken Feit observed, "The element of reluctance to prophesy seems absent from many 'prophets' today."[3]

---

[3]Ken Feit, radio interview. The program, called *Living and Free*, was hosted by Michael Thoms and was broadcast in California in the midseventies.

ONE-HANDED KNOT IN A ROPE

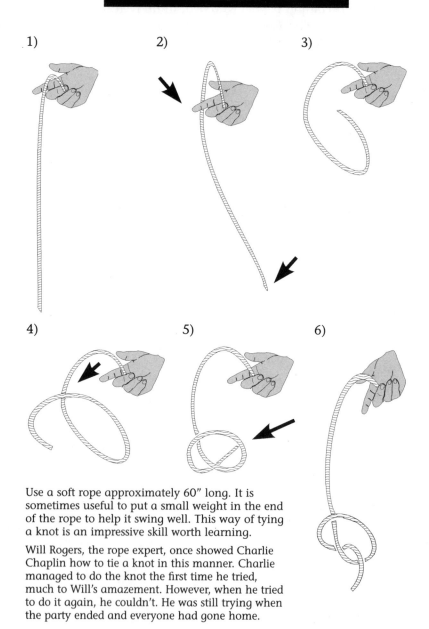

Use a soft rope approximately 60" long. It is sometimes useful to put a small weight in the end of the rope to help it swing well. This way of tying a knot is an impressive skill worth learning.

Will Rogers, the rope expert, once showed Charlie Chaplin how to tie a knot in this manner. Charlie managed to do the knot the first time he tried, much to Will's amazement. However, when he tried to do it again, he couldn't. He was still trying when the party ended and everyone had gone home.

CHAPTER 12

Magicless Magic

Links between various disciplines and art forms are often quite obscure, yet when they are discovered, they appear very obvious. The moment of insight may bring a fresh way of looking at a problem. For example, David Stein, faced with the problem of making large soap bubbles for his daughter, literally "dreamed up" the Bubble Thing which changed all their lives. Stein saw that there was no need to work with larger and larger frames. Instead, he chose to collapse the frame and dip it into the soap liquid. It could be expanded after being withdrawn from the container.[1]

This is an example of "magicless magic." The term was first used, as far as I can tell, by Margie Brown, an experienced American clown minister and teacher.[2] Magicless magic could also be expressed as *transforming the ordinary*.

Remember that God loves to work in mud, to take something (or someone) commonplace and show some new or unexpected insight. We find this throughout Scripture, where the weak and foolish ways of men are overwhelmed. Examples are David and Goliath, stuttering Moses, Gideon breaking pots and waving torches, the baby born in a stable, the uneducated fishermen chosen to be disciples, and "a God 'silly in the crib' and 'foolish on the cross.'"[3]

It is this very thing that first attracted me to origami, string games and soap bubbles, as these all involve transformation. A square of paper can be transformed into a bird with moving wings, and a string loop can become a snake that slips away into the long grass. Yet neither the paper nor the string is permanently changed. Both can be returned to their original

[1] J. Cassidy & D. Stein, *The Unbelievable Bubble Book* (Palo Alto: Klutz Publications, 1987), 73.

[2] Margie Brown, *A Clown Is Born* (San Francisco: self-published, 1982).

[3] J. Saward, *Perfect Fools* (Oxford: Oxford University Press, 1978), xi.

shapes, ready to be modified again. This relates to a branch of mathematics called topology.

Topology deals with the properties of surfaces which can be stretched and manipulated into different shapes. Such distortions are said to be topologicallly equivalent, as long as they can be returned to their original shape without cutting or tearing the surface. For example, there is no difference, topologically speaking, between an uninflated balloon and one tied at the neck and full of air. Even more surprising is the fact that the doughnut shape is topologically equivalent to the mug shape. Both are surfaces with one hole in them. This leads to the definition of a topologist as "someone who cannot tell the difference between a doughnut and a coffee cup."

A well-known puzzle[4] consists of gluing strips of paper into loops, adding various twists to the paper before joining the ends. The loop is then cut down the center and separated in two. But if the strip is given one twist before the ends are joined, the central cut gives one large, continuous loop. Two twists will give two interlinked loops. Why not experiment with this and try to find a story to fit the actions? This puzzle takes time to prepare. Quicker methods might be preferred for actual performance. Ideas already used include using material strips and tearing the band apart, or making the "band" out of a long zipper, with Velcro pads on the ends to fix and undo the same zipper with and without twists.

Another mathematical model that has great clown potential but has never been used, to my knowledge, is the Klein bottle. This is a one-sided surface and can be seen as a bottle with no inside.

If you do find a way of using these puzzles the following limericks might be of interest to you.

A mathematician confided
That a Möbius strip is one-sided,
And you'll get quite a laugh
If you cut one in half,

[4]W. Leitzmann, *Visual Topology* (London: Chatto & Windus, 1969), 110.

For it stays in one piece when divided.

A mathematician named Klein,
Thought the Möbius band was divine.
Said he, "If you glue
The edges of two
You'll get a weird bottle like mine."

The world view of the clown is always different from that of those around him. An unusual film made in 1980 by South African director Jamie Uys gives a wonderful example of this. *The Gods Must Be Crazy* tells the story of the meeting of two very different worlds. In the deep of the Kalahari desert, where no other race or tribe could survive, live the bushmen. They travel in small family groups, having little or no contact with the outside world. Into this simple life, where there is no concept of individual ownership, comes a present from the gods — at least it appears that way at first. A Coca-Cola bottle, thrown out of a low-flying plane, lands in the middle of the village. The tribe has never seen anything so wonderful before. It soon becomes a gift much cherished, useful for treating thongs, making music, pounding roots, holding water, printing patterns and a hundred and one other things. But the gods must have made a mistake, because there was only one bottle, and everyone needs to use it at the same time. Dissent, argument and even fighting breaks out. The gift is regarded as useless and the leader, N!Xau, throws the bottle back where it came from — into the sky. But the gods do not seem to want it either, and it falls back almost right on top of his head. That night the decision is made to drop the bottle off the end of the world, and so the little bushman sets out on his quest, which eventfully and eventually ends in success.

It appears that Uys ran into difficulties at the end of filming when he wanted to recompense the leading man, N!Xau. He realized N!Xau had no need or understanding of money when he discovered that the bank notes he had given him as pay had simply blown away. When asked what he would like as payment, N!Xau decided on twelve head of cattle. He had seen that they didn't run very fast when they were hunted. In the end, lions killed most of them, but the bushman and his clan did manage to "hunt" and eat the few left.

Many everyday objects contain within them the potential for magicless magic. A folding wood and cloth deck chair, such as used on the beach or on boats, can be a most creative prop. It can be easily carried, appears extremely difficult to set up, yet can be set up with one movement if lying flat properly. It can be not only a seat, but also a castle, a sail, a trap, a whale, a tent or a screen for you to change behind (with difficulty!). The chair may also appear to come alive if a length of fishing line is attached to it and it is pulled across the stage by an unseen helper positioned backstage.

Look at everyday articles and use your imagination. Turn them upside down, inside out or whatever. Itinerant fool Ken Feit used to suggest that we should begin this process by saying, "Ah, yes. I haven't seen one of these in a long time." Then we can go on to see a pair of glasses as firefighters for twins, or a pair of shoes as adjustable tear drop catchers for elephants to attach to their trunks. This way of creative thinking is coined "lateral thinking" by popular author Edward de Bono.[5]

It can lead us into great adventures in everyday life. Remember that just because everyone else thinks something, that doesn't make it right. Things are not always quite what they seem. There is more than one way of accomplishing most tasks, and usually one way is more fun than the rest. I recall my wife "creatively waking up" our teenage son who was going through a phase of finding it difficult to get up in the morning. After trying the usual methods to no avail, she took a bowl of dried peas, went outside into the garden and threw them, one at a time, at the bedroom window, until he got up to see what was happening.

Another idea that began as a clown thought has led to many happy days of balloon fishing. We haven't caught anything yet (other than people's interest), but it has been fun. Balloon fishing grew out of a desire to get a hand-line out into

---

[5]Edward de Bono, *Lateral Thinking: A Textbook of Creativity* (New York: Penguin Books, 1977).

deeper water beyond the seaweed while on vacation by the sea. Noticing there was a fairly constant offshore wind, we attached a balloon to the end of the line just above the bait and let the wind carry it out to sea. We quickly realized we needed more balloons to support the rest of the line as it went out, so every five yards or so, we attached a new balloon. Unfortunately, the baited hooks kept catching in the shallows, and after various trials and ideas, including trying to shoot the first balloon and burst it when it had gone far enough out to drop the bait deeper, we discovered a much better method. It involved a bit of preparation the night before, but it worked excellently. We took some baited hooks and a long length of fishing line and carefully wound them around an ice cube. Then we placed the ice cube with the bait and line into a drink carton, added some cold water, and put it in the freezer overnight to solidify. The carton kept any water from dripping out when we transported the ice block the next day. When we arrived at the fishing spot, we tore the carton off, then affixed the ice block, which floats, to the hand-line. Then the balloon was allowed to float off into the deep water, and within about five minutes, the ice melted, releasing the line and baited hooks to float gently down into the deep water. Why not try this the next time you go fishing?

The creative response that a natural clown makes in a tense situation carries no guarantee of a totally peaceful result, but it is likely that the story of the clown's response will be remembered and repeated, which could help to liberate and change people and attitudes.

The clown stimulates the imagination and opens up new possibilities because of his different view of the world. Though he may never accomplish the simplest of tasks, the fool expects to achieve things that mere mortals consider impossible. Ironically, the clown never fails, for he is living out a riskful adventure. While the way ahead is not mapped out, he can know the path, because it is always the one that rises, giving fresh challenges and wider and wider horizons to view as the journey proceeds. The adventure of living and loving holds many risks, but the only way you can fail is to refuse to travel.

Japan's most famous Christian novelist frequently writes on such themes, and not more powerfully than in his book *Wonderful Fool*. In this novel, Gaston, a descendant of Napoleon Bonaparte, visits Japan. He is not at all what his guests expect. He is large, "horse-faced," clumsy and poorly dressed. Neither does he appear to understand much of Japanese culture. He finds himself constantly misinterpreting people's attitudes, always believing the best of them. Toward the end of the novel, the main female character, Tomoe, comes to see Gaston in a new light.

For the first time in her life, Tomoe came to the realization that there are fools and fools. A man who loves others with an open-hearted simplicity, who trusts others no matter who they are, even if he is deceived or even betrayed, such a man in the present-day world is bound to be written off as a fool. And so he is. But not just an ordinary fool. He is a wonderful fool who will never allow the little light which he sheds along man's path to go out. It was the first time this thought had occurred to her.[6]

This is as good a definition of the Christian clown as I've come across.

◆

---

[6]Sushaku Endo, *Wonderful Fool* (Tokyo: Tuttle Publications, 1958), 180.

Part II

Clown Ministry Sketches

Introduction

The first part of the book explored some of the principles of holy foolishness. This second part consists of a collection of actual sketches in which the theory of clown sketch development is put into practice. This section includes a collection of ideas which have been used in audio-visual presentations in churches, theaters and in street performance.

The original material for these sketches comes from many different sources, including the Bible, traditional Jewish stories and proverbs, and local traditional tales.

Insights into everyday relationships, such as between strength and weakness, power and powerlessness, rich and poor, prove fertile soil for creating clown sketches. Simply juggling and thinking can stimulate the creative juices and suggest new ideas.

In the examples that follow, there are several ways of presenting the skits.

1) **Using a Narrator.** This has many advantages. It gives a clear and direct lead to the performers, and it provides an opportunity for some very entertaining ad-libbing. As mentioned before, pieces develop through performance and often need to be adapted to fit local situations. The sketch "Juggling Blindfolded" (page 165) developed through a whole series of performances. It began with the idea of a juggling puppet, and over the years has grown into a piece which is very well received by most audiences. Response can be predicted to some extent, but for the material to become effective, it is important to always be ready to respond to the unexpected.

The narrator should have a good, clear voice, as well as a confident and relaxed manner. If performing for large meetings, the narrator should know how to use a fixed microphone properly. Frequent practice is absolutely necessary for both the clown performers and the narrator. The narrator needs to be acutely aware of all the actions and antics that need to be accomplished by the performers so he can carefully time his delivery.

2) **Taped Commentary.** This is similar to working with a narrator. It is one of the best ways for solo clowns to broaden their material. It requires a great deal of patience and preparation to make the tape with the pauses in the right places and timed to the length required for each action. The sketch "The Juggling Lesson" (page 168) includes the timing after each statement to give a rough guide as to how the tape should be made. You may want to shorten or lengthen some of the times given, but this will give you a good basis from which to start. A great advantage to using prerecorded material is that the performance time can be known precisely, to the nearest second!

3) **Silent Mime.** This can be extremely effective in small amounts, but unless the clowns are trained and talented mime artists, it is best to keep these sketches very short and clear. It is a good idea to invite some sympathetic friends to review any mime sketch you are planning to present. Often the action that we feel is absolutely clear and obvious is totally confusing to others. The first lesson in mime is to keep presentations short and simple and to believe in the action you are doing.

4) **Speaking Clowns.** In the following sketches, there are several in which clowns are required to speak. The nature of the material does not require the clowns to have "funny" voices, though when this works well, it can be effective. The most important fact for speaking clowns to remember is that they need to speak out boldly in order to be heard. The timing of the words is also vital. Pauses in the right places can be extremely funny. You will get a feel for how to deliver your lines effectively through experience and practice.

5) **Music.** Introductory and background music can add wonderfully to a performance as a means of setting the atmosphere and keeping the rhythm of the performance. Again, as in the case of the taped narration of a clown sketch, it has the advantage that the exact length of the piece can be known and communicated to others involved in planning the event. It can be very unhelpful to overrun or underrun a clown performance.

Yet because of the nature of the interaction between the clowns and the audience, keeping to time can present problems. The use of music can ensure that you have enough time but not *too* much time. When the song ends, so does your routine.

Finding the right music may involve a great deal of searching and listening. When you find the music that you want to use, it is important to get permission from the copyright holder. A letter explaining exactly who you are and what you want to use the music for may well produce a positive and understanding response. Should copyright be a problem, it is worth asking musically gifted friends who have composition skills to write a piece especially for you. They will usually be glad to help, and they may also be able to produce some unusual sounds.[1]

6) **The End?** Finishing off or "styling off" is one of the first skills that circus performers teach their children. Knowing how to show that you are finished is an essential skill. While the end is usually straightforward when using taped material or working with a narrator, it is a little more difficult to discern in mime sketches. The clown, who is still on the performance area, simply faces the audience with feet together and arms raised to shoulder height to receive the applause. He then takes a shallow bow by bending at the waist and leaves the performance area.

Performance Rights

The author has graciously shared the clown sketches in this book for use by other clowns in ministry. Performance rights are granted with the purchase of this book, and no further permission is needed to adapt or integrate these sketches within any performance situation for clown ministry. However, sketches may not be reproduced, stored in a retrieval system, or transmitted, in any form or by any means, electronic, mechanical, photocopying, recording or otherwise, without permission of the publisher.

---

[1]At present, I am hoping to get a tape recording of a friend who plays the saw. The sound is very pure and unusual. I plan to use it as background to a presentation of soap bubbles.

TURNING THE HAND OVER
(WITHOUT TURNING THE WRIST)

This can be used as an introduction to many clown pieces and is a kind of "warm-up" exercise which encourages audience participation. It is particularly appropriate before the story of Noah with its biblical reference to the forearm or cubit as a "God-given" measuring tool.

CLOWN: Tonight I want to give you a free gift. It is something that you probably don't know at this moment, but when I have taught you, you will know it and be able to do it for the rest of your life. Maybe you will go home and teach others right away. I am going to show you how to turn your hand over without turning your wrist. *(The CLOWN turns his hand over, showing how the wrist is also turning at the same time.)*

Does anyone have any ideas about how to do it? *(Usually some ideas will be forthcoming. Among the good ideas suggested have been to turn a somersault or hold the hand straight out in front, then swing the whole arm out backwards. The CLOWN explains that the hand has to end up in the same place as it started.)* I'll show you how to do it. Watch my wrist carefully to make sure it doesn't turn. *(The CLOWN now makes the moves as shown on pages 119 and 120 calling out, "One, two, three..." and so on at the completion of each step.)*

Now the hand is upside down. Let's do it together. *(Usually everyone is willing to do this, but should some adults be hesitant, add...)* Why don't you give it a try? You know you'll go home and try it anyway! *(Again the CLOWN goes through the steps, calling out the numbers as all the audience members move their forearms in unison.)*

Let's run through it again and see if you can remember how to do it. *(The process is repeated once again. The CLOWN calls out the numbers and encourages the audience to accomplish this new skill.)*

Practice that twice before you go to bed tonight and once tomorrow when you get up, and you will never forget it.

(You may find that someone will point out that the wrist never actually turns at ANY time, rotation only takes place in the elbow. Graciously thank them for this information and go on to the next piece.)

TURNING THE HAND OVER
(WITHOUT TURNING THE WRIST)

Instructions

1.

Begin with the hand palm up at about waist level, as if carrying a plate.

2.

Bending the forearm at the elbow, bring the hand up, so that the fingers point at the ceiling.

3.

Allow the forearm to fall across the body so that the hand lies flat as if about to pat the stomach.

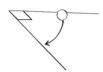

4.

Continue the movements as in step 1. Notice that the hand is now at a right angle to the starting position.

5.

Repeat movement as in step 2.

6.

The hand is now turned over and all that remains to be done is to move it, sideways, back to the starting position.

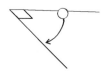

The hand is now turned over.

7.

CHAPTER 13

Old Testament Clown Sketches

ADAM AND EVE

(Genesis 3)

CAST: One Clown.

PROPS: One large white juggling ball, two multicolored juggling balls of the same size, one large ripe tomato with the green stem still attached, one green "pencil" or 260-type balloon (the kind used for balloon art, available at clown supply shops), two small green bags to fit the juggling balls and some green thread.

SETTING: A tomato is suspended by green thread from any convenient bar or frame at Stage Left, at about head height. The green balloon is hidden in a suitable place. The clown has one multicolored ball in each pocket. The two greens bags to fit the juggling balls can be suspended close to the tomato with a clothespin that can quickly be undone. The white juggling ball is centrally placed. It sits on an appropriate small stand or table. (This symbolizes God resting on his throne. I set the white ball on a small, highly polished brass candlestick.)

(When the sketch begins, the CLOWN enters and stands beside the table with the white ball on it.)

CLOWN: **God made the world...** *(Indicates the white ball.)*

...and saw that it was good. *(Lifts white ball off the stand and moves it about slowly, as if the ball was looking all around the performance area. The ball is returned to a still position on the palm of the left hand.)*

But God felt sad that he alone could appreciate this wonderful creation. *(Lowers ball about two inches.)*

Then he had a wonderful idea. *(Throws white ball eight inches into the air, straight up from the left palm.)*

He thought, "I know what to do. I'll make a little self-image." And that is exactly what he did. *(Puts white ball into left-hand pocket, and after a brief pause, takes white ball out again, along with the multicolored ball that was in that pocket. Places white ball in right hand and the colored ball in left hand, holding the hands at waist height, palms upwards.)*

And God was very happy with his creation. *(Throws white ball a little into air and catches it in the same hand. Then the colored ball is similarly thrown into the air, but a little lower than the white ball. Repeats this several times with the white ball clearly going higher than the colored one.)*

Every day they would play together endless games of all sorts, from soccer to crossword puzzles. *(The two balls now change from hand to hand, as in two-ball juggling. Make several different patterns.)*

Yet no matter what the game or the sport, God won hands down. If they played soccer, God always won; sometimes ten to one, sometimes eleven to one, or even twelve to zero. When it came to crossword puzzles, God always finished them in thirty seconds. After a few days of this, the little self-image became very sad, and God, being God, noticed. *(Stops the two-ball juggling and holds the balls in separate hands as at the beginning.)*

"It just isn't fair," said the little self-image. *(Raises the hands holding the multicolored ball when it "speaks.")* "You always win."

"I'm so sorry," God replied. "I just didn't think. *(Raises the hand holding the white ball when it speaks.)* I'll make sure you win next time we play, and I'll go extra slow on the crossword puzzle."

"No, that isn't any good. I'll know that you aren't

really trying." *(Raises the multicolored ball again.)*

God paused and thought, and once more he had a great idea. He made another self-image. *(Leaving multicolored ball in position, puts the white ball in the right-hand pocket and then draws out the other multicolored ball along with the white ball.)*

Truly this was a wonderful creation, and everyone was overjoyed. *(Begins to juggle the three balls, and on the word OVERJOYED, throws the balls in the overthrow pattern for one cycle.)*

Every day God made a trip around the world, and then returned each evening to share with his self-images. *(Juggles the multicolored balls together in one hand. The white ball is removed behind the back for a moment to symbolize God's "trip around the world." The white ball is then returned to the pattern and three-ball juggling starts again.)*

Then one day when God was away, a stranger arrived. *(Puts the white ball in the left-hand pocket and moves over to where the green balloon is hidden. Produces the balloon slowly with a hissing sound.)*

The stranger then asked the two self-images all about themselves, and they eagerly told him all that had happened. The stranger asked, "SSS...did God say you were allowed to eat everything you want?"

"Yes," they replied, "everything except the fruit of that tree over there." *(The CLOWN points toward the tomato suspended at Stage Left.)*

The stranger suggested sneakily, "Perhaps it might just be that this God you were telling me about doesn't want you to win at soccer or to be able to complete crossword puzzles more quickly than he does. Perhaps that fruit might make you just as clever." *(Returns green modeling balloon to its original place and places one ball in each hand as before.)*

The first self-image said to the second, "God didn't

say that we weren't to look at the tree, did he?"

"No," replied the second. And so they went to look. *(The CLOWN carries the two balls over to the tomato.)*

The second self-image said, "God never said we weren't allowed to pick the fruit of the tree, did he?"

"No," replied the first self-image. *(Picks the tomato with the right hand using a twisting motion, to make sure it comes away cleanly.)*

The first self-image said, "God never said we weren't to kiss the fruit, did he?"

"No," replied the second. *(Raises tomato to lips and kisses with a light kiss.)*

"One little bite can't do any harm, can it?" asked the second.

"I'm sure not," the first agreed. *(Juggles tomato along with the two balls as this is being said, and then makes several false starts before the tomato is finally bitten firmly and the juggling stops. Since the tomato is ripe, the bite will make a bit of a mess and will be quite noisy. The CLOWN pauses as he slowly becomes aware of the consequences of his action.)*

Then they heard the sound of God coming back. *(CLOWN makes anxious movements, moving the balls to various inappropriate hiding places. Finally the CLOWN pulls the two little green bags down from the clothespins and stuffs a ball into each. He lets them rest on the palm of his right hand. Then he brings the white ball out of his right-hand pocket and allows the ball to "look around.")*

God saw the little self-images huddling in the greenery and asked them, "Why are you hiding there?"

"We're not hiding, we were just…" they attempted to reply, but their voices were muffled by their coverings. God brokenheartedly said, "You have to leave here. You have fallen for a lie." *(On the word FALLEN, the two juggling balls are dropped to the floor.)*

Then God turned and looked around *(CLOWN now*

moves back to the hiding place of the green balloon) **and called the stranger out.** *(The green balloon is drawn out reluctantly.)*

And as God considered exactly what to do about the sad situation, the seed of an idea began to form in his ever-creative mind. *(The CLOWN folds the balloon into a z shape with one of the ends being longer than the other and gives a twist to form a cross.)*

NOAH

(Genesis 6-8)

CAST: Narrator, Noah and two Clowns.

PROPS: One large square of paper, a set of large cards with animals on them (there needs to be a duplicate card for each animal in the pack), two dishes of strong bubble liquid, two bubble wands, a net, two white birds and two black birds (instructions for making the birds are on pages 130-132), large leaf (real or made from green construction paper).

(NOAH [who may be dressed in a biblical-style robe] is alone in the center of the performance area. The large sheet of paper [pre-creased as shown on page 129] lies to his right, and the pack of large animal cards is at his left. Two dishes of strong bubble liquid with a bubble wand are On-stage — one at the left and another at the right of the performance area.)

NARRATOR: **Noah was a good and holy man who listened to God.** *(NOAH does not react to the words "good" or "holy," but tips his head to one side attentively on the word "listened.")*

And God said, "Build me a wooden boat." *(NOAH looks around and sees no wood.)*

God said, "GO FOR [gopher[1]] wood." *(NOAH goes for wood. He moves to the large piece of paper and with some puzzlement turns it over and over. He looks around for some measure, then "notices" his forearm with surprise. He finds he has a similar measure at the end of his other arm, and that they are exactly the same length. Now using some of the moves which were taught in "Turning the Hand Over (Without Turning the Wrist)" [page 117], and using the creases that are already there, he folds the paper into a boat [per the instructions on page 129].)*

God told Noah, "Now find two of each kind of animal to take with you in the boat." *(CLOWNS now begin a giant game of cards with audience participation. The large cards are shuffled and laid face down on the performance area. The*

[1]See Gen. 6:14.

CLOWNS *now take turns trying to "find" pairs of animals by turning over a couple of cards at a time. If the cards match, they are then taken over to the boat and tucked inside. If they do not match, the cards are turned back down and left in the exact same position. The* CLOWNS *may make some very silly decisions as to which cards to turn over. The audience is encouraged to help them find the pairs. Finally the pairs are all placed in the boat.* CLOWN 1 *notices the two black birds and captures them with a net. They are also put into the boat.* CLOWN 2 *captures the two white birds and coaxes them into the boat.*

(Now NOAH *notices the first drops of rain, holds out his hand to check the raindrops and hurriedly mimes climbing into the boat. He then hides behind it.*

(The other CLOWNS *stand in a line with their hands in fists raised high and out in front of them. The backs of the hands are uppermost. The* CLOWNS *now symbolize rain falling by opening their fists, allowing the fingers to point downward and wiggling them slowly back and forth while slowly lowering their hands. This is repeated several times.)*

Then after forty days, the rain stopped and Noah came out. *(*NOAH *comes out from behind the boat.)*

He could only see water in all directions, and so to find out if there was any dry land, he released a black bird. *(*CLOWN 2 *takes one of the black birds from the boat and gently moves the wings back and forth.* CLOWN 2 *moves to the left and right of the performance area, always getting farther and farther from the boat. Finally* CLOWN 2 *disappears from sight.* NOAH *strains his eyes, looking for the bird.)*

Then Noah decided to send another bird. *(*CLOWN 1 *takes one of the white birds from the boat and "flies" it back and forth in front of the boat. He then comes to* CLOWN 2 *who has reappeared, holding the large leaf behind his back until the bird comes close. Then* CLOWN 1 *takes the leaf on behalf of the bird and returns to* NOAH.*)*

And the bird came back with evidence that the

waters were truly going down. Noah praised God for his wonderful deliverance. *(NOAH praises God with appropriate gestures.)*

And God sent a sign in the heavens to all his people of his love for them.

(CLOWNS 1 and 2 stand, one behind the other, facing outward.

(CLOWNS 1 and 2 move in unison as follows: CLOWN 2 bends to the left, lifts the bubble wand out of the bubble liquid, and slowly waves a long tube of bubble in an arc from left to right. CLOWN 2 bends to the right, lifts the bubble wand out of the bubble liquid, and slowly waves a long tube of bubble in an arc from right to left. This makes a rainbow for an instant before bursting.)

NOAH

Paper Prop Instructions

BOAT

1. Use a large square of brown paper. Fold the top to the bottom, then open out. Fold the left side to the right side, then open out.

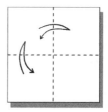

2. Fold in half diagonally, then open out. Fold in half in the other direction diagonally, then open out.

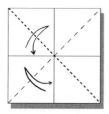

3. Fold each side in turn into the central fold line, then open out.

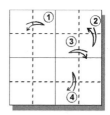

4. Pinch each corner as shown.

5. Arrange the flaps as shown to make Noah's boat.

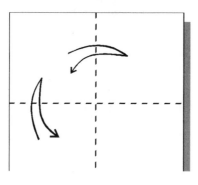

6. Hold the fold in place with clothespins.

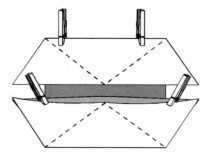

BIRDS

1. Fold the square of paper along the horizontal and vertical axes, and along one diagonal axis. Open out.

2. Turn the paper over and fold in the remaining diagonal fold.

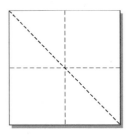

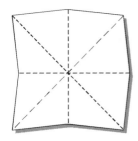

3. Using these folds, bring the four corners of the paper together and press flat.

4. Position the paper as shown, with the center of the paper farthest away. Fold the two flaps into the center of the diamond as shown.

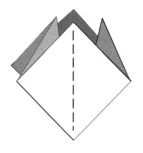

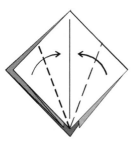

5. Turn over and repeat the same folds on the two flaps on the other side.

6. Fold the triangle based on the center of paper, down as shown and then back again.

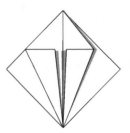

7. Open out the
newly folded flaps
to stand vertically.
Peel off the top
layer of paper and
move this upward.

8. In process...

9. Turn over and
repeat this.

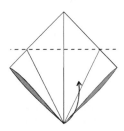

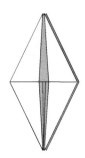

10. With the thumb and index
finger, move one point
upward, reverse-folding
one of the points.

11. In process...

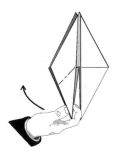

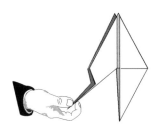

12. Complete.

13. Repeat with the other point.

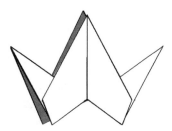

14. Make a small reverse fold on one point as shown.

15. Complete.

16. Hold the base of the bird as shown with the thumb and fingers of the left hand, and gently pull the tail with the right hand. The wings should begin to flap. If they do not, "loosen" the folds by making and remaking the bird along the same lines. Gently pull again.

17. Pre-crease two white and two black squares in preparation for the sketch.

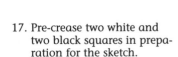

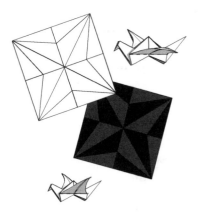

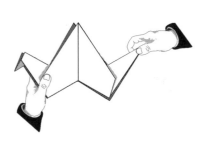

JONAH

CAST: Narrator and Solo Clown.

PROPS: See pages 137 to 142 for construction of paper props.

(A large newspaper (1) lying at Stage Left, with a smaller folded "ticket" [prepare some newspaper by folding it into the shape shown in (2) as far as the step (2) (h) ready to become the boat.] Also at Stage Left, lay a roll of paper ready to become the tree (14) and a pair of scissors with "eye" which represents the mite (16). A folded newspaper in the form of a boat (10), lies on the right of the stage, ready to become the big fish and a string of folded paper figures which are to be held up at the end of the sketch (18). The CLOWN has a pocketful of confetti to be thrown over the boat at (3).

NARRATOR: *(Recites the following with appropriate pauses for the CLOWN to act.)*

Now Jonah, son of Amittai,
Heard the Lord's command:
"Go to Nineveh at once,"
But he chose to flee the land.

He scanned the local paper *(1) (CLOWN opens out the large newspaper.)*
For a cruise ship going West
And finally bought a ticket *(2) (Picks up "ticket" (2) (h) and opens out, to give boat.)*
And set out on his quest.

Not many days had passed
When a storm hit the ship. *(3) (Rocks the boat back and forth and throws confetti on it.)*
It blew, it rained, it hailed and snowed,
The decks were all aslip.

The captain called the crewmen *(4) (Makes the captain's hat (2) (c) from the boat and puts on the hat.)*

To clear out all the hold,
And as the storm grew greater,
They did as they were told.

"If anyone down there has faith,"
The captain hailed the men,
"Then now's the time to pray,
And say a loud *amen*." *(5) (Joins hands as if in prayer.)*

But Jonah called to the captain, *(6) (Beckons to the hat shape.)*
"You must throw me in the sea.
I'm running from the God of heaven,
And he ain't pleased with me!"

The captain then protested, *(7) (Wears the captain's hat.)*
"But you'll drown right away!"
Yet as he talked, the boat broke up. *(8) (Turns fold back into boat and tears off the top, bow and stern off the boat.)*
He knew Jonah could not stay.

So Jonah, to the watery depths
Seems gone forever now.
"Life jackets on!" the captain cried, *(9) (Unfolds what is left of the boat to give the life jacket.)*
"The boat has lost its bow."

But wait! A giant fish appeared *(10) (Makes the fish shape, using the paper at the right side of the stage.)*
And with one mighty bite,
Swallowed up poor Jonah whole —
His chances now seem slight.

With three days gone, the big fish swam
To a bay with a sandy beach.

It coughed and wheezed and spat him out, *(11) (Opens the fish's mouth.)*
Land was within his reach.

Thankful for his life again
And recalling God's request,
"All right, I'll go to Nineveh,
I think that might be best!" *(12) (Turns and walks back to starting place.)*

For three whole days, poor Jonah preached.
He didn't go to bed. *(13) (Mimes preaching and walks up and down.)*
The people turned away from sin
And accepted what he said.

So Jonah left the city
Feeling rather glum.
He was very cross with God
For all that he had done. *(13) (Sits down, looking unhappy.)*

"I knew it all the time, great God,
This didn't have to be.
You can do almighty things.
Did you have to pick on me?"

Tired and weary, he lay to rest,
In a deserted spot,
Shaded by a baby tree, *(14) (Holds roll of paper vertically.)*
He found it not too hot.

God graciously increased the shade *(15) (Draws center of the roll up to its full height.)*
And made the tree grow high,
And Jonah's spirit lifted,

And he gave a grateful sigh.

But at night, a mite began to bite, *(16)* *(Cuts the tree with the scissors into little pieces at first.)*
And killed the tree stone-dead,
With a crash, the palm tree fell, *(17)* *(Cuts through the main trunk. Paper tube falls on his head.)*
Right onto Jonah's head.

Now Jonah grew quite angry!
He raised his fist and cried,
"Why do you play such games with me?
You know how hard I tried."

And then God spoke to Jonah,
A message clear and true,
If you care so much for an oil palm,
Shouldn't I care as much for you?" *(18)* *(Pulls out string of paper people.)*

Paper Prop Instructions

1. Large Newspaper

(a) Twelve pages of newspaper are stuck together with transparent tape into one large sheet. To do this, you will need to find a large, flat area of floor or table on which to work.

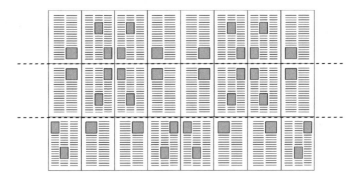

(b) Accordion-fold the large newspaper.

(c)   (d)

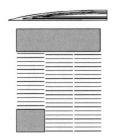

2. Boat

(a)

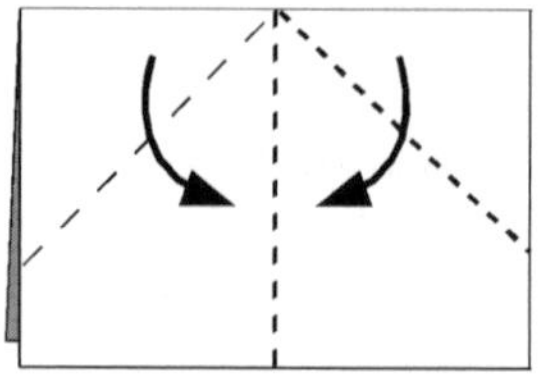

(b)

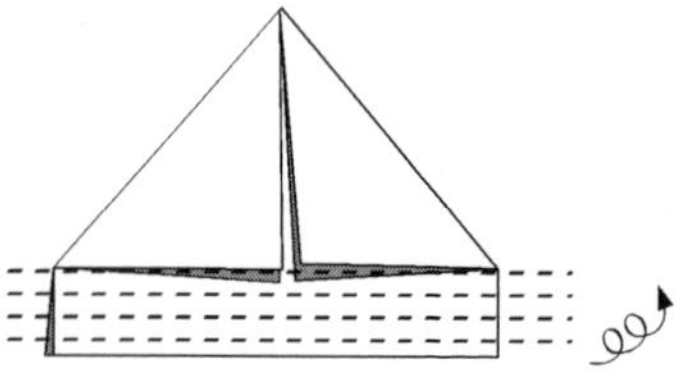

Repeat behind

(c)

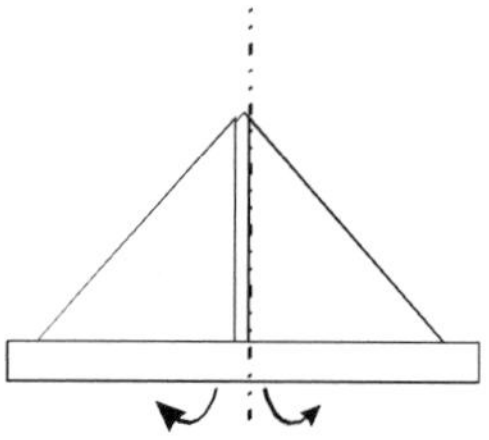

Captain's hat

(d)

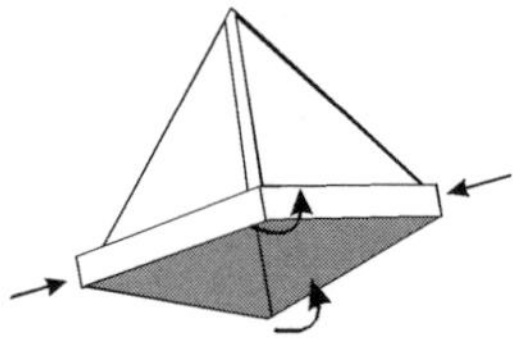

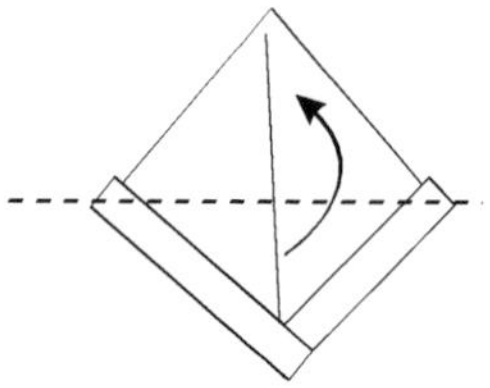

Repeat behind

(e)

(f)

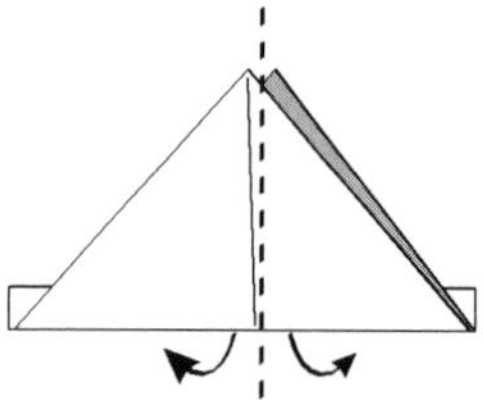

(g)

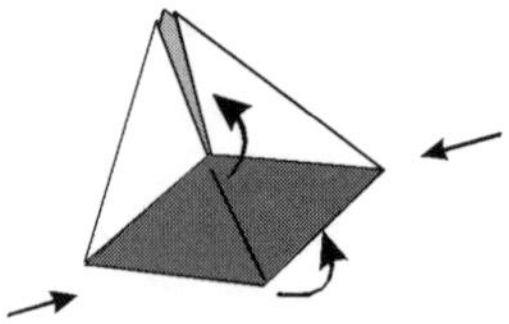

(h)

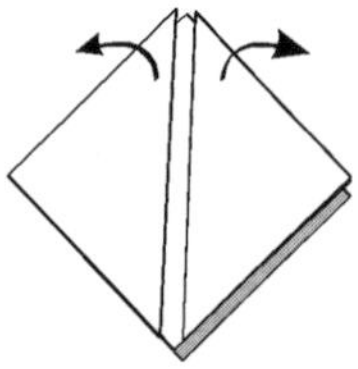

(i)

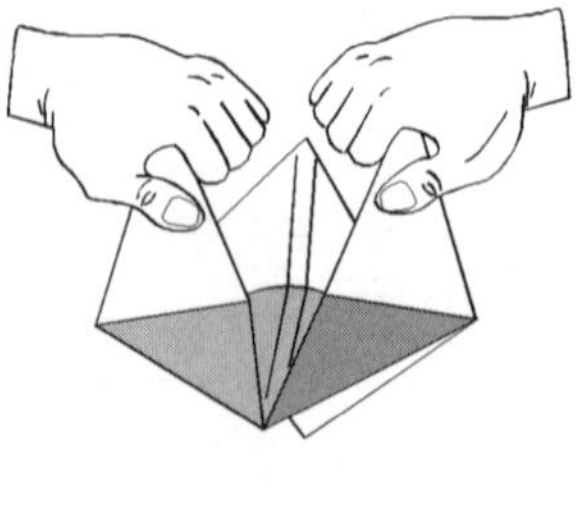

(j) Boat

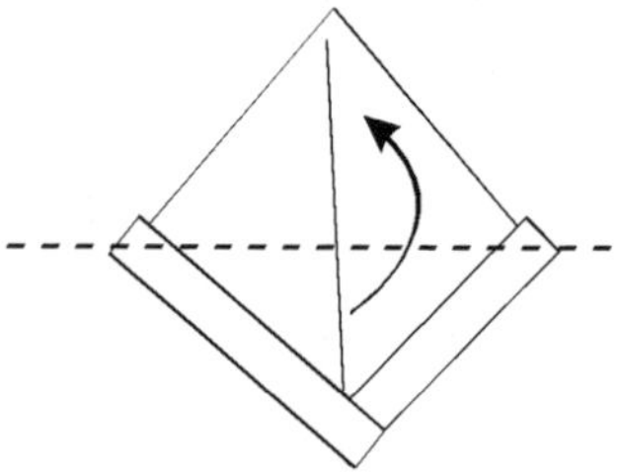

8. Life Jacket
To make the life jacket, tear the boat as follows:

(a) First the bow,   (b) then the stern,

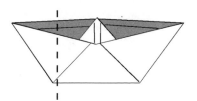
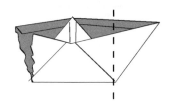

(c) and finally the center point.   (d) Now open it out...

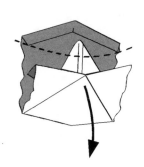
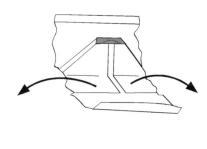

(e) ...to give the life jacket.   (f) If made large enough,
                                           it can be worn.

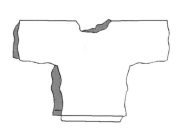
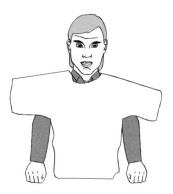

10. Giant Fish

(a) Make the giant fish from a previously prepared paper boat.

(b) First, fold the center point of the boat flat against one side.

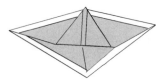

(c) Then fold the bow to meet the stern, keeping the boat shape intact.

(d) Now the mouth of the fish can be opened and closed.

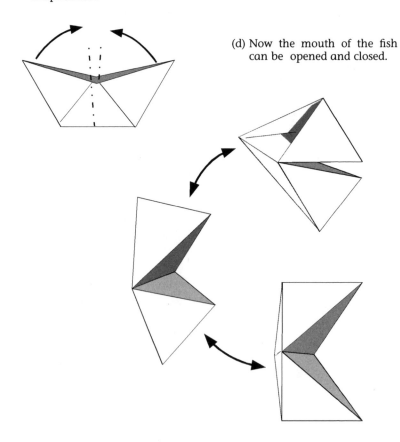

14. Palm Tree

(a) To make the tree, tape five sheets of newspaper together in a strip and roll them into a tube.

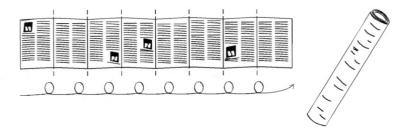

(b) Cut the end of the tube at 1" intervals to a depth of 6" as shown below.

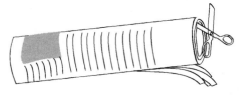

(15) By pulling the center of the roll out little by little, the tree can be extended to full height.

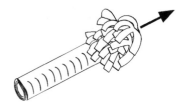

(16) A large "eye" is added to a pair of scissors to make them look like the little mite.

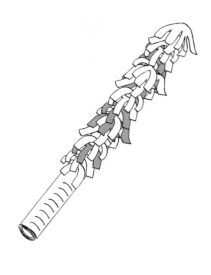

17. Paper People

A strip of newspaper 2 yards long is accordion-folded and then cut as shown below.

(a) Strip of paper.

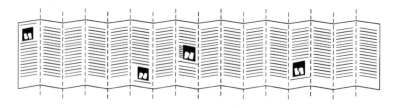

(b) Folded up.

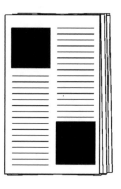

(c) Cut to this pattern.

(d) Extended.

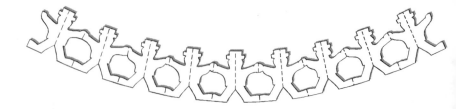

CHAPTER 14

New Testament Clown Sketches

THE SOWER

(Adapted From Mark 4)

CAST: Narrator (or taped commentary) and Solo Clown.

PROPS: About 2 yards of soft, yellow cord.

(CLOWN stands in the center of the performance area. The right hand holds one end of the cord, the left hand, the other end.)

NARRATOR: There was once a sower who went out to sow.

(The CLOWN raises the cord and lays the ends over the right and left shoulders respectively, and with the left hand, lifts up the center of the cord to make the sowing basket. The right hand casts the seed left and right out into the audience as the CLOWN walks back and forth across the performance area.)

Some of the seed fell along the path...

(Removes cord from around neck and makes the "seed" as shown on pages 145 and 146 under the title "The Path." Pause at step 7.)

But the birds of the air came and ate them all up.

(The CLOWN makes a "clucking" sound like a hen and pulls the string to release the false knot on the words "ate them all up.")

Some of the seed fell on rocky ground, where it did not have much soil.

(Makes the pattern entitled "The Rocky Ground" on pages 147 and 148, up to step 8.)

The seed soon sprouted, because the soil was shallow.

(Continues to make step 9 of the pattern.)

But when the sun came up, the plants soon withered,

because they had such tiny roots. And they didn't produce any seed.

(Continues with steps 10, 11 and 12.)

Other seed fell among thorns...

(Make the pattern entitled "The Weeds" on pages 149 and 150, up to step 6.)

which grew up and choked the plants, so that they did not produce any seed, either.

(The CLOWN coughs loudly when the NARRATOR says the word "choked," and continues with steps 7, 8 and 9.)

Still others fell upon good soil.

(Makes the design entitled "The Good Soil" on pages 151 and 152, up to stage 5.)

It came up, grew and produced a crop, multiplying thirty and sixty and one hundred times.

(Continues with stages 6 and 7.)

Then Jesus said, "Those who have ears to hear, let them hear."

(The CLOWN points to his ear, then out to the audience, and nods.)

THE SOWER

The Path

1. Hold the cord as shown. Move the right hand to the left BEHIND the left arm, and drape the cord over it, without pulling tight.

2. Move the right hand, from behind, into the hanging loop, and catch the central string on the back of the right arm.

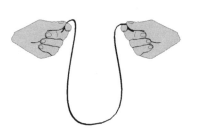

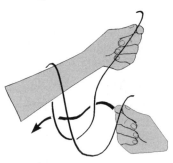

3. Move the right hand back to the starting position and pull tight.

4. Lift the loop off the back of the left wrist and pull the string tight.

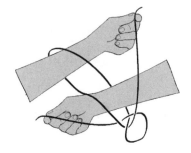

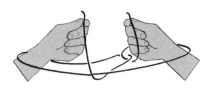

5. In process.

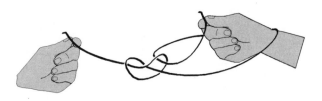

6. Now lift the loop off the right
   wrist and slowly pull the
   string until the central "knot"
   is quite small.

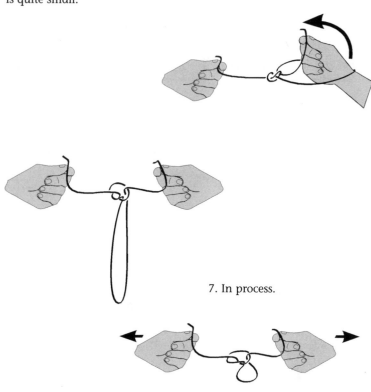

7. In process.

8. Finally, pull the string. With a little
   pressure, the "knot" disappears.

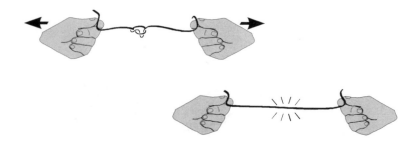

The Rocky Ground

1. Hand the cord over the left hand.

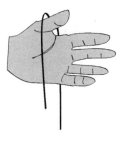

2. With the right index finger, draw out the string hanging down the back of the left hand, between the left thumb and index fingers.

3. Twist the loop clockwise one half turn, and place the loop over the index finger.

4. With the right index finger, draw out the string hanging down the back of the left hand between the left index and middle fingers.

5. Twist the loop clockwise one half turn, and place the loop over the middle finger.

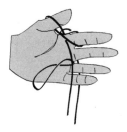

6. Repeat this same process, this time drawing out the string between the middle and ring fingers and placing the loop on the ring finger.

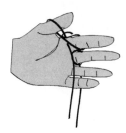

7. Repeat the process, drawing out the string between the ring and little fingers of the left hand. Place this loop on the little finger.

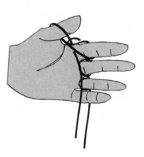

8. Lift the loop off the thumb and draw up the string.

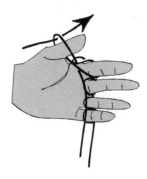

9. The loop is now fully extended.

10. Release the loop and let it fall over the hand.

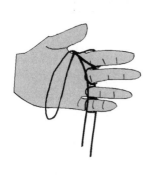

11. With the right hand, pull the end of the cord, which hangs from the near side of the left hand.

12. Complete.

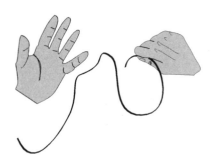

The Weeds

1. Hold the cord between the hands as shown, left-hand fingers pointing away, right-hand fingers pointing toward the body.

2. Now move the hands together, turning both palms toward the body. The right hand moves *behind* the left hand.

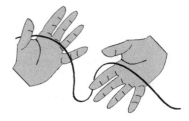

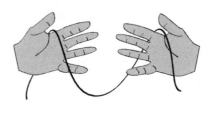

3. Take hold of the string that is hanging down the back of the left hand with the tips of the right index and middle fingers while simultaneously taking hold of the right-hand string with the tips of the left index and middle fingers.

4. Move the hands apart, allowing the loops to drop off the palms, but keeping firm hold with the index and middle fingers.

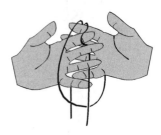

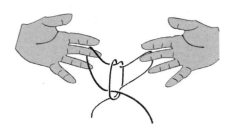

5. With the thumbs, spread open the loops.

6. Draw the ends of the cord up through the loops.

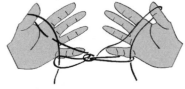

7. Drop the loops held by the
   index and middle fingers,
   holding tight to the ends of
   the cord.

8. Move the hands so that the
   left hand is vertically above
   the right hand, and slowly
   draw the hands apart.

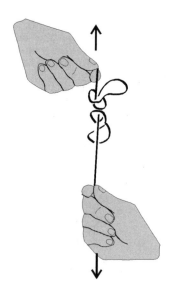

9. Complete.

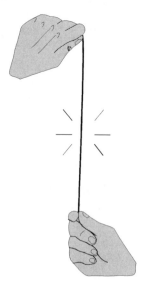

The Good Soil

1.

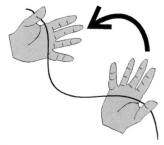

Hold one end of the cord in the left hand between the thumb and the index finger, with the left hand pointing to the right with palm facing in.

With the right hand, lift the cord a few inches from the held end, and twist the string so that the end hangs behind the short loop between the hands.

2.

Lay the cord onto the left hand with a half turn inward. This allows the longer hanging end to hang down the left palm as shown. Do not pull tight.

3.

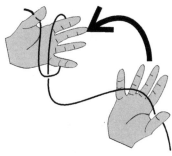

Repeat move 1. This time, grasp the cord a few inches farther away from the left hand.

4.

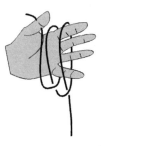

Repeat move 2. This second loop must be kept separate from the first and will be slightly larger.

5.

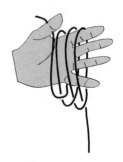

Repeat moves 1 and 2. Again, the loop should be a little larger than the previous one. Do not pull tight.

6.

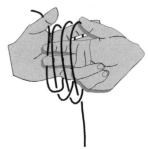

Pass the right index and middle fingers through the three loops and grasp between them the end of the cord, which is being held between the left thumb and index.

Release the hold of the left-hand fingers, and draw this end back through the loops.

7.

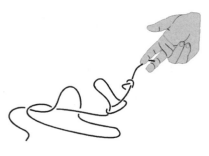

Allow the loops to fall off the left hand.

8.

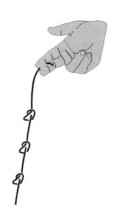

Complete.

THE PARABLE OF THE TALENTS
(Matthew 25)

CAST: Four Clowns, one of whom must be proficient at juggling three balls, (and Off-stage Voice).

PROPS: Six juggling balls in a small bag, a handkerchief and a large collection of juggling and clown equipment, such as clubs, unicycle, hoops, stilts and costume pieces.

NOTE: This sketch may either be performed as a mime sketch, or with appropriate words of dialog added as necessary (see Scripture).

(Three CLOWNS stand in a row facing the audience, spaced three yards apart. The fourth CLOWN is the landowner and carries the small bag with the six juggling balls in it.)

CLOWN 4 enters and looks the three CLOWNS up and down, then carefully moves toward CLOWN 1, shaking his hand. He gives him three balls from the bag.

CLOWN 4 continues to CLOWN 2 and gives him two juggling balls.

CLOWN 4 continues to CLOWN 3 and gives him one juggling ball. He then leaves the performance area, waving good-bye to the three clowns.

CLOWN 1 examines the juggling balls and begins to experiment with them, slowly throwing and catching, throwing and missing, and slowly getting the hang of it. After some time, he is able to juggle fairly smoothly. He then stops contentedly and rests.

During all this, CLOWN 2 and CLOWN 3 watch CLOWN 1 carefully.

Then CLOWN 2 looks at his two juggling balls, and with some difficulty begins to juggle two balls in one hand. Satisfied, CLOWN 2 then stops juggling and rests also.

CLOWN 3 now looks at his juggling ball and tires to get brave enough to throw the ball in the air. He treats the ball as if it were made of glass. He also shows great concern over the possibility of getting the ball dirty, and he lays a handkerchief down on the floor where the ball might fall, should he fail to catch it. Even when he kneels down on the ground to reduce the possibility of the ball dropping a long way, he cannot bring himself to let go of the ball. Finally, he carefully wraps the ball in the handkerchief and puts the handkerchief containing the ball on his head (under his hat) "to keep it safe." He appears uneasy and worried.

CLOWN 4 happily returns, loaded down with clown equipment, e.g., stilts, clubs, hoops and unicycle.

He then shakes hands with CLOWN 1 and asks to see the balls he had given him. CLOWN 1 shows the balls and juggles well. CLOWN 4 is delighted, and proceeds to give this clown an abundance of the equipment that he brought with him.

He then moves on to CLOWN 2, greets him enthusiastically, and asks to see the juggling balls. CLOWN 2 juggles two balls in one hand. CLOWN 4 gives him a further two balls and encourages him to practice juggling two balls in both hands. (This can end up with four-ball juggling if the CLOWN is proficient enough.)

CLOWN 4 now moves on to CLOWN 3 and asks about the juggling ball. Looking quite pleased with himself, CLOWN 3 produces the juggling ball, which is wrapped in the handkerchief, from under his hat.

CLOWN 4 shows his disapproval and snatches back the juggling ball. He gives it to CLOWN 1.

CLOWN 4 then points Off-stage, and CLOWN 1 slowly walks off hanging his head.

VOICE: *(From Off-stage)* **Do not store up for yourselves treasures on earth, but store up for yourself treasures in heaven. For where your treasure is, there your heart will be."**[1]

---

[1]Matthew 6:19-21, author's paraphrase.

THE LOST SHEEP

(Inspired by Matthew 18:12-14 and Luke 15:4-7)

CAST: One Narrator, one Clown.

PROPS: An easel and the sheep cards (instructions on page 157).
*(The shepherd CLOWN is holding the four large sheep cards.
The smaller sheep square is hidden somewhere, e.g., on the
floor or behind the easel.)*

NARRATOR: **Daily a shepherd brought his sheep** *(Shepherd
CLOWN shows his sheep. He lays cards a, b, c, and d upon the
easel as pictured in diagram 1.)*
In from the mountain fields to sleep.
Called each one home by its own name
Always in order — always the same.

He settled them within the fold, *(CLOWN now carefully lifts
the cards off, one at a time.)*
One hundred sheep — safe from the cold
Till morning of the next day came,
And then he let them out again.

And so it was, as the weeks passed, *(CLOWN assembles the
sheep cards again as per diagram 1, and takes the cards off as
before.)*
The cuddly sheep, well-fed, grew fast.
They wandered over hills and dales,
And ran home nightly, wagging tails.

Then one evening, sad to say, *(CLOWN assembles the cards
again, but this time as per diagram 2. A square central hole will
appear.)*
A little lamb wandered away.
The shepherd didn't sleep that night,
But searched the hilltops till first light.

Then spied him lying 'neath the brush, *(CLOWN discovers*

the "missing" sheep. This fits exactly into the center hole.)
Picked him up, and in a rush,
Brought him back where he belonged,
Snugly fitting in the throng.

The lost is found, there's no more need *(CLOWN gives the little lamb a pat.)*
To worry — or to buy a lead,
For from now on he'll never stray.
The lost lambkin is home to stay.

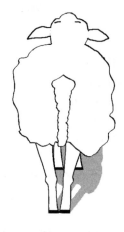

THE LOST SHEEP

Sheep Card Instructions

The shapes may be constructed out of thick cardboard or plywood. It is best to make this as it will appear when finished (i.e., diagram with sheep square in place). This will ensure a neat fit when the lost sheep is finally restored to its proper place.

It is important to draw the sheep at different angles to each other. This helps to give the impression that the finished shape is the same as the original one. It is important that you mark the corners very carefully so as to be able to find the right way to assemble the picture — both to show the fold full of sheep and also with one missing.

Begin with the four pieces assembled as in diagram 1.

As the story continues, the pieces are split up and reassembled again as in diagram 1.

Then, when the sheep is lost, the pieces are assembled as in diagram 2. This will show a missing hole in the center.

The small square has been previously hidden somewhere within the performance area. The shepherd clown searches all over the place until finally coming upon the lost sheep (square).

He then returns it to its proper place as the poem ends.

To show this story to the best effect, it is helpful to have an easel on which the pieces may be assembled.

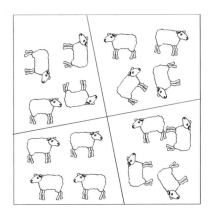

Diagram 1

Diagram 1

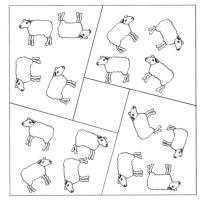

Sheep Square

CHAPTER 15

Clown Sketches From Jewish Traditional Tales

THE TWO BROTHERS

CAST: One Narrator, two Clowns of different size and shape.

PROPS: None.

(The NARRATOR is standing to the left of the stage and ideally has memorized the text. The two CLOWNS enter and stand facing the audience. They stand some three yards apart and respond to the text as the NARRATOR speaks.)

NARRATOR: **Once there were two brothers who farmed together.** *(The two CLOWNS step forward in unison, smiling and pointing first to themselves, and then to each other. Then, in unison, they make the movement of digging and turning over the soil three times, then casting and sowing three times. They then scythe the crop, in unison, three times.)* **And they shared equally all that they had.** *(The CLOWNS carefully gather together their part of the cut crop and make a special point of gathering up to the center line of their half of the performance area.)* **Now one of the brothers, the younger one, was single and lived all alone,** *(The larger CLOWN indicates that he is the youngest and takes one step forward)* **while the other was married with five young children.** *(The smaller CLOWN steps forward, counts out the number of his children on his fingers and smiles happily.)*

The younger brother thought to himself, *(YOUNGER CLOWN adopts thoughtful pose and slowly taps the side of his temple with his index finger, tipping his head slightly to one side.)* **"It is not fair that I should farm half of the land and half of the crop when I have only one mouth to**

feed and my brother over there *(He points to OLDER CLOWN, who is apparently unaware of him at this moment)* has a wife and many children to support. But I know him. *(The YOUNGER CLOWN taps the side of his temple with his index finger and nods sagely.)* He is too humble to accept anything."

And then he had a wonderful idea. *(The YOUNGER CLOWN shows surprise and wonder on his face and moves from a thoughtful pose into a bright, excited one.)* Beginning that very night, as soon as it was dark, he went to his own barn, *(The YOUNGER CLOWN moves to the back of the performance area and to the side, where his "barn" is, and mimes opening the door and entering)* picked up a sack of grain, and carefully and quietly carried it over to his brother's granary. *(The YOUNGER CLOWN mimes picking up a very heavy sack of grain and, tiptoeing slowly, carries it across the stage, behind OLDER CLOWN. He carefully opens his brother's barn door and puts the sack of grain inside. The YOUNGER CLOWN now returns to the position he was in at the beginning, alongside OLDER CLOWN, who has never moved throughout all this and has apparently been oblivious to all that has been said or done. The CLOWNS look at each other, giving a brief, friendly nod, then both look to the front.)*

The older brother, having just finished his evening meal and having enjoyed the wonderful family time, began to consider his younger brother, and he thought to himself, *(The OLDER CLOWN turns slowly and looks at the YOUNGER CLOWN out of the corner of his eye.)* "It's not fair that I have half the farm and half the crop when I have a wife and five lovely children, *(Again he counts the children on the fingers of his hand as the NARRATOR speaks)* yet my poor young brother has no wife or family to support him in his old age. But I know him. *(The YOUNGER CLOWN taps the side of his temple with straight index finger and slowly nods sagely.)* He is too humble to accept anything."

And then he had a wonderful idea. *(The OLDER CLOWN also shows surprise and wonder on his face and moves from a thoughtful pose into a bright, excited one.)* **Beginning that very night, as soon as the children were all in bed, he went to his own barn,** *(The OLDER CLOWN moves to the back of the performance area and to the place where the YOUNGER CLOWN had carefully carried his sack to, where his own "barn" is. He mimes opening the door and entering)* **picked up a sack of grain, and carefully and quietly carried it over to his brother's granary.** *(The OLDER CLOWN mimes picking up a very heavy sack of grain and tiptoes slowly across the performance area behind YOUNGER CLOWN. He carefully opens his brother's barn door and puts the sack of grain inside. The OLDER CLOWN now returns to the position he was in at the beginning, alongside YOUNGER CLOWN, who has never moved throughout all this action. The CLOWNS look at each other, giving a brief, friendly nod, then both look to the front,)***

And so both brothers fell asleep, feeling satisfied with the work of the day...and of the evening, also. *(They breathe more deeply and allow their heads to fall forward.)*

In the morning, when the brothers woke up, the first thing they did was check how much space they had left in their barns. *(The CLOWNS both stretch and yawn, rubbing the sleep from their eyes. Unaware of each other, they turn to their barns, open the doors and count the number of sacks they have.)* **What a surprise! Both of them had exactly the same number of sacks as they had at the end of yesterday's work.** *(After some puzzlement, they look happy and begin to rejoice, again not aware of each other.)* **And they thanked God for his great and wonderful goodness.** *(The CLOWNS both turn their eyes upward and raise their hands in praise to God. They then return to the starting position, standing side by side.)* **This went on day after day,** *(Repeat the actions from * to ** without the commentary, somewhat* *more quickly)* **week after week.** *(Repeat from * to ** a third time very rapidly indeed, returning to the starting position.)* **And every morning, they found that their barns were just as full as they had been the night before.** *(The CLOWNS pause, then turn to check that their barns are in fact full and return, satisfied.)*

But one night, the younger brother was late in setting out, and the elder brother decided to make the trip *before* his meal instead of after. *(The CLOWNS go through the same actions from * to **, but this time they are both moving at the same time.)* **And...the brothers met!** *(They pick up their sacks and slowly move toward each other. They move stealthily, with their backs toward each other, until they finally bump into each other.)* **They were so surprised to see each other.** *(The CLOWNS show surprise.)* **And then they noticed the sacks of grain that each carried.** *(Indicate with pointing and puzzlement.)* **And then it dawned on them.** *(The CLOWNS show emotion of recognition of the situation.)* **They smiled and laughed and embraced,** *(The CLOWNS embrace, cheek to cheek. Holding this embrace, they smile at the audience)* **and God looked down from heaven, and he smiled and said, "This is a holy place, because there has been much love here."** *(On the word holy, the CLOWNS jump apart and look directly at the spot on which they were standing. They look up at the NARRATOR, then back at the spot. They remain still for some time before leaving the performance area.)*

GOD IS TO BE PRAISED

CAST: Narrator (who is also the king in the story), and two Clowns.

PROPS: A King's crown, several long French loaves, two large chocolate coins covered with golden paper. One of the loaves has large slits cut in its base in which to conceal the coins. One red magic marker.

(The NARRATOR, standing Stage Left, wears the crown. He is the king in this story and describes the events as they happen while the CLOWNS act out the story. A container stands before the king in which the loaves of bread are completely hidden.)

NARRATOR: **Two beggars come here every day, and you know how it is.... We kings like to do our best to help the needy.** *(The two CLOWNS enter from the right side of the performance area, and the NARRATOR/KING graciously bends down and pulls out a loaf of bread for each of them from the container in front of him. They cross to the NARRATOR.)*

CLOWN 1: **Thank you, O King.** *(He bows low before the NARRATOR and receives the bread.)*

CLOWN 2: **Thank you, O God.** *(He does not bow to the NARRATOR, but steps back and raises his hands in the air in praise and thanksgiving. CLOWNS exit to the right, again happily talking together.)*

NARRATOR: **It is hard to be generous when some people, like that clown, just don't appreciate you. I asked him once why he didn't thank me properly. Do you know what he had the audacity to say?** *(Mimicking)* **"Well, if God hadn't given it to you, then you wouldn't have been able to give it to me!"** *(NARRATOR scratches his head, and then has a moment of revelation.)* **I'm going to teach him a lesson tomorrow.** *(NARRATOR leaves and then returns, thus symbolizing the passing of one day. When he returns, he carries two large, golden coins. He carefully places the coins in the loaf with the slits on the bottom and arranges them before him so that he cannot possibly muddle them up.*

He does, of course, forgets several times, and mixes them up by mistake. Finally, he marks the one with the coins with a large red spot on the end which faces the audience. The CLOWNS enter exactly as before.)

NARRATOR: **Good morning, my good fellows. Here you are.** *(He hands over the loaves as before, playing to the audience by noticing the red spot in a much-exaggerated manner, then giving them a knowing wink.)*

CLOWN 1: **Thank you, O King.** *(As before, he bows low before the NARRATOR and receives the bread.)*

CLOWN 2: **Thank you, O God.** *(As before, he doesn't bow before the NARRATOR, but steps back and raises his hands in the air in praise and thanksgiving. This time they move back to the right-hand side of the performance area a little more slowly, then CLOWN 1 stops and turns to CLOWN 2.)*

CLOWN 1: *(Weighing his loaf in his hand, he then notices with horror the red spot on the end of the loaf. Looking to make sure his fellow clown hasn't seen it, he quickly puts his hand over it.)* **Do you think our loaves are all right today?**

CLOWN 2: **Yes. Why do you ask?**

CLOWN 1: **Mine feels a bit heavy and doughy, and you know that I have such a tender stomach.** *(He says this in such a way as to convey to the audience that he is obviously tricking his fellow clown.)* **Do you think we might swap loaves today?**

CLOWN 2: **Of course, my friend. Whatever you wish.** *(The CLOWNS exchange loaves and CLOWN 1 hurries off. CLOWN 2 stays, sits down, and prepares to eat. He says grace.)* **Thank you, God, that you provide so generously for our every need.** *(He breaks the bread, and out falls the two large, golden coins.)* ***Thank you, God!***

CHAPTER 16

Clown Sketches That Use Juggling Skills

JUGGLING BLINDFOLDED

CAST: A Glove Puppet and one Clown.

PROPS: Three juggling balls and a blindfold for the puppet.

CLOWN: I want to introduce you to a very special friend of mine. *(CLOWN goes over to his case or suitable box and coaxes out the PUPPET with gentle words of persuasion. Finally the PUPPET agrees to come out.)*

His name is _____, and he is rather shy. *(The PUPPET turns his head into the CLOWN and hides himself away from the audience. He is extremely bashful. Again, with much persuasion, he is encouraged to feel that the audience is indeed very friendly and wants very much to meet him.)*

But _____ has a very special talent that is rare among little creatures of his age. He can *juggle*! *(Again the puppet turns away, but not quite so quickly this time; and he is more easily persuaded to turn back to the audience.)*

But he doesn't juggle in the usual way. He juggles while lying on his back. *(Hold out the PUPPET, lying on his back. This will, in fact, be the normal starting position for juggling for the CLOWN. Usually the adults realize this and laugh, while the children are still expectant to see what the PUPPET can do)*

Now if any of you think this is easy, just you try juggling while lying on your back. It is very difficult. I should also explain that _____ can juggle excellently, but I am not very good. So if any of the balls fall, don't blame _____. It will be my fault entirely.

(Now put two juggling balls into your left hand and one into the PUPPET's grip.) **Can you count with me for ten throws and then give a good clap for _____? He would be very encouraged.** *(Juggle the balls in standard pattern for ten throws, trying to emphasize how good the PUPPET is and how hesitant the other throwing/catching hand is. Pause for applause, letting the PUPPET take the bows.)*

(The PUPPET now turns to the CLOWN and comes close to whisper in the CLOWN's ear. The CLOWN listens intently.) **Are you sure?** *(The CLOWN asks the PUPPET. Again, a whispered conversation takes place between the CLOWN and PUPPET, and the CLOWN finally announces:)* **Ladies and gentlemen, boys and girls, I am proud and excited to present a very special event. _____ wants to try a seldom-performed feat. He is going to try to juggle while blindfolded.** *(Pause a little at this point. The adults will usually find this funny while the younger children will be full of anticipation. Hand blindfold to a nearby adult.)* **Can you please check this blindfold to make sure that there is no way that anyone can see through it?** *(Take back the blindfold as it is confirmed to be what it purports to be.)* **It is important to check also that the blindfold is properly attached, for there are some disreputable performers who actually cheat by peeking out of the bottom of the covering. Can you please help by attaching the blindfold to your complete satisfaction?** *(Another person is asked to attach the blindfold precisely.)*

Now we need absolute silence, for the way that _____ accomplishes this amazing feat is by listening very carefully to the sound of the juggling balls being caught and thrown. Here we go again. Please count on your fingers this time, and when we get to ten, give a big cheer for _____. *(Now begin to juggle. Stop at three throws and ask everyone to be absolutely silent, even stopping breathing if they can. Juggle ten times and take the* *blindfold off the PUPPET. He then takes a bow to applause of all.)*

NOTES: When putting the puppet away, cradle him in your arms and place him carefully back in the case or box. It is possible to destroy the whole illusion by simply pulling off the puppet and throwing it to one side.

The puppet I use for this sketch is a small, furry baby kangaroo which we found "forlorn and lonely" under the driver's seat of a moving van. Though he is now somewhat threadbare and a little old, he does have a very attractive appearance.

It might be a good idea to find someone who can make good, simple glove puppets and request that one be made especially for you. This special puppet will be quite unique, and you can develop special routines for him along the lines of the above, with the puppet being the clever achiever and the clown being the somewhat less-expert helper.

A puppet is especially useful in the event that any small child becomes distressed by the appearance or actions of the clown.

THE JUGGLING LESSON

I developed this sketch for solo performance and have used it for over a decade in all kinds of performance settings. It was developed from the closing line, and then a full introduction was added as follows. It could, of course, be successfully developed with a narrator as the teacher instead of the tape. The following is the script that I use on the cassette tape, but it may be varied to accommodate the particular skills and tricks with which the juggler is most proficient. It is important to be sure that all the tricks are well within the skill level of the performer.

CAST: Solo Clown (and Off-stage helper to operate the tape recorder).

PROPS: Three juggling balls, prerecorded cassette tape and a tape recorder, speaker.

(There is a speaker visible at the right side of the performance area from which the taped monolog can be heard. The three juggling balls are placed at the extreme left of the area, ready to be found by the CLOWN. He enters smilingly and stands in the center of the performance area. The tape is started and the voice speaks.)

NARRATOR: **Hello!** (15 seconds)

(The CLOWN reacts to the voice and finds that it is coming from a box [loudspeaker] which is in full view of the audience. CLOWN mimes a greeting.)

So you want to learn to juggle, do you? (5 seconds)

(CLOWN nods his head enthusiastically.)

All right. Go and get those balls over there. (10 seconds)

(The CLOWN looks all around, then moves slowly to the left side of the performance area.)

No, right over there. (5 seconds)

(The CLOWN now notices the three juggling balls laying at the edge of the area. He picks up one of the balls.)

Go ahead, then. (5 seconds)

(CLOWN stands, holding one of the balls in his hand in the

beginning position. He waits.)
To juggle, you have to throw the ball. (5 seconds)
(The CLOWN throws the ball about two inches high and catches it. He turns to the speaker and looks for approval.)
Higher than that. (5 seconds)
(The CLOWN throws the ball about six inches high and looks at the speaker for approval.)
Try even higher, and keep going. (15 seconds)
(The CLOWN throws the ball to the proper height and catches it several times. He is very pleased with himself.)
That's good, but that's not juggling.
(The CLOWN looks disappointed.)
Try throwing the ball over to your other hand. (10 seconds)
(The CLOWN positions his left hand alongside his right and carefully throws the ball over the gap of about two inches between his hands.)
Higher than that. (5 seconds)
(The CLOWN does as he is asked.)
Now, keep on going. (15 seconds)
(The CLOWN continues to throw the ball from one hand to the next, getting more and more confident.)
But that still isn't juggling.
(The CLOWN looks sadly at the speaker.)
Pick up a second ball and place it in your other hand. (5 seconds)
Now, change them over. (10 seconds)
(The CLOWN does as he is asked, placing one ball into each hand. He changes them by passing the balls from one hand to the other without throwing.)
No, not like that. You have to throw the balls. (10 seconds)
(The CLOWN pauses, then does as he is asked, throwing the first ball and catching it in the other hand alongside the second ball, then throwing the second ball back to the empty hand, keeping the first ball where it was caught.)
You must throw both the balls. (15 seconds)

(The CLOWN now throws the balls one after the other and begins to accomplish the next step. He is very pleased with himself.)

But that's still not juggling. You need another ball. Go and pick it up and put two balls in one hand and one in the other, and off you go. (10 seconds)

(The CLOWN does as he is asked, though he shows some disappointment at continually being unappreciated. He now juggles as before, simply keeping the third ball in the palm of one hand secured by the little finger.)

Not like that. You must throw all three balls. (10 seconds)

(The CLOWN pauses, puts his hands close together and throws all three balls into the air, and looks again at the speaker for approval.)

Look! Just throw the three balls, one at a time, from one hand to the other. (15 seconds)

(The CLOWN takes a deep breath and does this successfully.)

Don't stop — keep going. (10 seconds)

(The CLOWN continues, at first jerkily, then slowly getting smoother and more accurate.)

Why not try something different? (10 seconds)

(The CLOWN now throws one ball straight up and catches it in one hand while still juggling the other two in the other hand.)

Good! Anything else? (10 seconds)

(The CLOWN now crosses his hands as he continues to juggle.)

Now try throwing one straight up and two over the top. (15 seconds)

(The CLOWN tries this and fails spectacularly, dropping all three balls. He stands still, dejectedly looking at the floor.)

Oh! You dropped the balls. Never mind — just pick them up and try again. Dropping balls is not a sign of clumsiness. It can be a sign of growth.

(The CLOWN tries again with some hesitation, and then succeeds well. He takes a final bow.)

Clown Sketches From Various Sources

THE SNOWFLAKE

CAST: Narrator (either live or taped) and solo Clown.

PROPS: One large, rectangular sheet of white paper; one pair of scissors.

(CLOWN makes snowflake during narration using the instructions on pages 173 and 174.)

NARRATOR: It was winter, and the clouds were heavy and white. *(CLOWN holds out paper as per Step 1.)*

On the summit of a very high mountain, there was a rock, and on the very tip of the rock, the first flake of snow fell. *(CLOWN folds paper as in (2).)*

He was soon joined by his brothers and sisters, who covered the whole mountain; and they happily spent the winter together.

As he was waking up, the snowflake began to think to himself, "What will people think of me, a mere snowflake? Anyone looking at this mountain will see that I am above everything else. I have no right to be in such an exalted position. It would be no more than I deserve if the sun looked at me and melted me, just as he did some of my brothers and sisters." *(CLOWN begins to snip paper as per (3).)*

After some thought, the snowflake decided, "I know! I will escape the sun's anger by going down to a level more fitting for someone of my size."

The little snowflake jumped off the top of the mountain *(CLOWN cuts the tip off the paper as in (4))* and began to roll down the mountainside. But the farther he rolled, the bigger he became. *(CLOWN rolls snowflake as in (5).)* Soon he became a giant snowball, which came to rest at the foot of the mountain.

And so it was that in the summer, the snowflake lived longer than any of his brothers and sisters, and was the last of all the snow to melt in the sun. *(CLOWN opens snowflake as in (6).)*

THE SNOWFLAKE

Origami Instructions

(1) Hold the large sheet of paper out almost horizontally to represent a cloud of snow.

(2) Fold the paper as shown to give a shape like a pointed mountain as below.

(a)

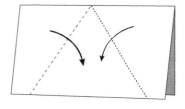

(b)

(3) Begin to cut little shapes out of the paper as shown below to illustrate melting snow. Let the pieces of paper fall to the ground.

(4) Cut the very tip of the paper mountain and watch it fall to the ground.

5. "Roll" the paper down toward the ground by turning it over and over in the hands. Also, slowly open it out at the same time, but keep it horizontal when it is fully open.

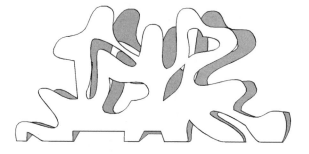

(6) Now hold up the paper to reveal the large snowflake.

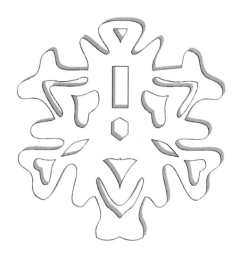

LIKE SHEEP

(A Mime Sketch)

CAST: Four or more Clowns.

PROPS: One bench; one tray like walking vendors at athletic events use, with a cord fastened to it that goes around the neck (the tray can thus be carried without having to use the hands); the tray holds three small plastic telescopes; one large floppy hat or similar distinctive piece of clothing; small basket, saucer and several large coins.

CLOWN 1 sits on the bench, staring upward at one particular point on the ceiling without moving. After several seconds, CLOWN 2 enters, walking past CLOWN 1 across the performance area from left to right. CLOWN 2 nods a greeting to CLOWN 1 as he walks past. CLOWN 1 takes no notice at all. He keeps staring upward at the same spot. CLOWN 2 now returns somewhat inquisitively and quietly sits down beside CLOWN 1 and looks up at the same spot on the ceiling, screwing up his eyes to try to see what CLOWN 1 is so engrossed in.

CLOWN 3 enters from Stage Left and nods a greeting toward CLOWNS 1 and 2. He also goes past them and then slowly returns to sit next to them on the bench, looking up at the same spot.

CLOWN 4 enters and goes through the same procedure. He

ends up sitting beside the other three CLOWNS on the bench. They all stare intently at the ceiling.

CLOWN 1 slowly steals a glance at the other CLOWNS and very quietly moves away, slipping off the bench and leaving the performance area to the right. He returns a few moments later "in disguise" as far as the other clowns are concerned, but still obviously the same clown to the audience. (For example, he may be wearing a big floppy hat.)

CLOWN 1 now carries a salesperson's tray with three telescopes on it. He is about to wander past the three CLOWNS on the bench when CLOWN 4 notices him.

CLOWN 4 crosses to CLOWN 1 "in disguise" and buys a telescope, reaching deep into his pocket and paying with several coins. The coins are placed in a basket with a small porcelain saucer in the bottom of it so they make a loud noise as they are dropped in.

CLOWN 3 hears the noise of the coins dropping and moves toward the salesperson. At the same time, CLOWN 4 returns to the bench and begins to train his telescope on the spot on the ceiling that they have all been staring at. CLOWN 1 notices this, and in mime inquires of CLOWN 4 where he got his telescope. CLOWN 4 points toward CLOWN 1, who by this time is now selling a telescope to CLOWN 3. Again, a noisy exchange of coins takes place.

CLOWN 2 rushes up to join the line. When it is his turn, he, too, eagerly pays for his telescope in coins.

CLOWNS 2, 3, and 4 go back to their same positions on the bench and train their telescopes on the spot. They now become animated, pointing and sharing with each other about the things they are seeing.

CLOWN 1 gives the audience a knowing wink and leaves via the left side of the performance area.

CLOWN 1 returns from the left, this time without his "disguise." He is jingling the coins in his pocket with as much noise as possible.

CLOWNS 2, 3, and 4 stop looking at the ceiling and turn their gaze on CLOWN 1. They look at each other, and then at the telescopes in their hands. By this time, CLOWN 1 has disappeared from the performance area to the left. There is a loud sound of a sheep from Off-stage: "Baa! Baa!"

(It could be even more effective to conclude by playing a short tape of sheep bleating.)

JEWELS OF THE KINGDOM
(Mime Sketch)

CAST: Five Clowns.

PROPS: One package, carefully wrapped in a large sheet of paper, which contains three large, fake jewels; one velvet bag or other special container; one large envelope labeled "Insurance Policy;" a large sign reading "Safe for Sale," and a large box decorated to look like a safe.

(The wrapped package containing the jewels is set in the center of the performance area on a small table.)

CLOWNS 1 and 2 enter from the left, conversing happily. They then notice the box, and CLOWN 1 goes forward quickly and picks it up and begins to unwrap it. A large piece of paper is discarded. CLOWN 2, who is quite happy not to interfere, picks up the paper that has been thrown aside and folds a paper bird.[1] CLOWN 2 exits to the left, happily playing with his paper model.

CLOWN 1 continues to open the box and is delighted when he finds the three jewels. He greedily grabs them, then realizes he cannot go through the rest of life carrying them. He looks around to see where he can put them, and just then CLOWN 3 enters from the right, carrying a very attractive velvet bag. CLOWN 1 negotiates to buy the bag from CLOWN 3 and gives him a jewel in exchange for it. CLOWN 3 exits to the left. CLOWN 2 now puts the remaining jewels into the bag and continues to grasp the bag very tightly.

CLOWN 4 enters from the left, carrying a sign which reads "Safe for Sale." CLOWN 1 approaches CLOWN 4 and agrees to buy a safe. CLOWN 4 exits, then returns carrying the safe (which is apparently very heavy). He walks over to CLOWN 1, who pays him with a jewel out of his velvet bag. CLOWN 1 opens the safe and puts the velvet bag in, yet he shows he is still greatly concerned by his actions.

CLOWN 5 enters from the right and notices the concern of CLOWN 1. He reaches into his pocket and produces a large

---

[1]See the instructions for making the paper bird following the sketch entitled "Noah" (page 130).

envelope titled "Insurance Policy." He opens it, shows the document to CLOWN 1 and appears to explain all the conditions to him. CLOWN 1 opens the safe, removes the bag and pays CLOWN 5 with a jewel from the bag (CLOWN 1 does not realize that this is the last one). CLOWN 5 exits to the left, showing great satisfaction.

CLOWN 1 is a little happier now and prepares to walk off to the right, then decides to check his great wealth before going. Opening the safe, he removes the bag. He then opens the bag and is shocked to find it empty. He turns it inside out and begins to search everywhere for the missing jewels. CLOWN 1 continues to search everywhere around the performance area.

CLOWN 2 now returns and walks across the front of the performance area with the folded paper bird. He is totally engrossed as he slowly flaps the bird's wings.

The sketch ends with CLOWN 1 still searching everywhere around the performance area.

TO RECEIVE A HEART

CAST: Five Clowns.

PROPS: Each Clown has a large pocket attached to his costume over his heart. CLOWN 1's pocket holds a medium amount of "stuff," including a cut-out heart shape. CLOWNS 2 and 3 have the greatest amount of stuff in their pockets, with brightly colored handkerchiefs hanging out over the tops. CLOWN 4 has a medium amount of stuff. CLOWN 5 has nothing in his pocket. Also needed is a large sign with "HEART TO GIVE AWAY" written boldly on it.

CLOWN 1 sits cross-legged in the center of the performance area, holding the "HEART TO GIVE AWAY" sign. CLOWNS 2 and 3 enter from the left, laughing and chatting happily. Their heart pockets are bulging and full to overflowing. Brightly colored handkerchiefs hang out over the tops of them. They pass by the seated CLOWN 1, scarcely noticing him. Then CLOWN 2 turns back. Obviously thinking that CLOWN 1 is begging, he selects a little colored handkerchief from his bulging pocket. CLOWN 2 tucks the handkerchief into the pocket of CLOWN 1, giving him a friendly pat on the shoulder. CLOWN 1 tries to protest, but CLOWN 2 has gone on his way, still laughing and chatting with his friend. CLOWNS 2 and 3 leave to the right.

CLOWN 4 enters from the left. His pocket is not as full as that of CLOWNS 2 and 3. He pauses and looks at the sign. CLOWN 4 shows some interest, but as he touches his pocket, he appears happy enough to go on with what he already has. He leaves to the right.

CLOWN 5 enters from the left. He is the slowest moving of the clowns. His pocket is completely flat and empty. He approaches CLOWN 1, and they enter into mime discussion. CLOWN 1 dips into his pocket and pulls out the heart shape. He gives is to CLOWN 5, who puts it into his pocket with joy. CLOWN 1 gets up and links arms with CLOWN 5, and they exit together.

LABELS

(Mime Sketch)

CAST: One smartly dressed Clown and up to nine other Clowns.

PROPS: A set of cards with strings attached so that they can be hung around the necks of Clowns 2-9, reading: FATHER, SON, HUSBAND, BOSS, EMPLOYEE, BROTHER, FRIEND, BREADWINNER; one love balloon (a heart-shaped balloon that is available at clown supply shops and some gift shops); one pair of scissors.

Love Balloons

CLOWN 1 enters, looking happy. He is then greeted by CLOWNS 2-9, with CLOWN 1 adopting the relationship that his label communicates. As each CLOWN leaves, he hangs his label around the neck of CLOWN 1. CLOWN 1 sags a little as each new notice is added. He is finally almost bent double by the weight of responsibilities.

CLOWN 10 enters with the love balloon tied to the back of his belt and a pair of scissors sticking out of his pocket. CLOWN 10 crosses to CLOWN 1 and shows genuine concern for his heavy weight of labels. After trying to lift the labels off, he realizes that there is a quicker way and produces the pair of scissors. CLOWN 10 cuts the strings holding the labels, and they quickly fall off. CLOWN 1 straightens up and shows delight and relief.

CLOWN 10 gives the love balloon to CLOWN 1, who is naturally delighted. All CLOWNS enter and rejoice together. They begin to have a party. CLOWN 10 slips quietly away.

BALLOON CAPTURE

CAST: Several Clowns.

PROPS: Some helium-filled balloons, a child's bow and arrows, a fishing rod, a length of transparent fishing line and a roll of transparent tape.

(The helium-filled balloons are tied together in a bunch with string. The balloons are in the highest part of the ceiling of the meeting place before the performance begins. A string with a loop on its end hangs down from the bunch of balloons, but it does not come down far enough for anyone to reach it easily. There is also a further connection to the balloons by means of a transparent fishing line which is loosely fixed at the back of the performance area, well out of the way.)

The CLOWNS enter and notice the balloons. They then experiment with various ways of trying to get ahold of the string. One tries to jump up, then balances on the shoulders of another clown. Another begins to organize a human pyramid with disastrous results. None manage to get high enough to reach the string.

Then one CLOWN, thinking hard, realizes that the only thing holding the balloons up is the helium. He shows this in mime to the others. He then looks for a heavy weight to pull down the balloons. He takes a heavy clown boot and tries to throw this through the hanging loop, knowing that its weight will be sufficient to bring the balloons down. This doesn't work either.[1]

Another CLOWN, picking up on the same idea of the helium being the only thing holding the balloons up, goes and gets a bow and some arrows and prepares to shoot the balloons, so as to be able to reach the string. The others hurriedly stop him.

A further attempt is made by the smarter of the big CLOWNS, who goes off from the performance area and returns with a fishing rod. He assembles this confidently, and sure enough, the tip just reaches the string loop. The impression

[1]It might just happen that by chance the boot does, in fact, catch the loop and bring the balloons down. If it does, finish the sketch there and gratefully accept the amazed response of the audience, acting as if this was what was intended all along!

should be given to the audience that this is really the way the sketch is supposed to end. However, each time the tip of the rod touches the string loop, the string swings away out of reach. It soon becomes evident that this method will not succeed either.

Throughout all the attempts of the clowns to bring the balloons down, the SMALLEST CLOWN has been tugging at one or another, trying to attract their attention. This becomes more and more noticeable as the different methods are tried. Now that all the other CLOWNS are finally at a loss as to what to do, the SMALLEST CLOWN moves to the center of the performance area and asks the others to pay attention. Everyone stops and looks at the SMALLEST CLOWN. Slowly and deliberately, he walks to the back of the performance area and takes hold of the fishing line, which up to this point should have been invisible.

The SMALLEST CLOWN gently begins to pull on the line. The balloons come down slowly, until the string is within easy reach of the SMALLEST CLOWN. The other CLOWNS turn and applaud the SMALLEST CLOWN as he grabs the balloons, then they joyfully take the balloons and distribute them throughout the audience.

A Second Method of Retrieving the Balloons

You will need tape, some extra helium-filled balloons as "rescue" missiles, and some string.

Cut several lengths of tape (approximately four inches long) and make them into loops by sticking one end to the other, with the sticky side of the tape outward. Stick several of these loops all over the upper parts of the rescue balloons. Attach a light string to each rescue balloon, and allow them to float up to the balloons in the roof.

As the balloons with the sticky tape touch the other balloons, a strong enough contact can be made to pull down those that were out or reach. By gently pulling on the length of string, all the balloons can be retrieved. Three "rescue" balloons should be enough to pull down up to ten linked helium-filled balloons.

The Rainbow Sins[1]

One day, which happened to be a Thursday, a most strange thing happened. All over the world, at 11:40 a.m., a fine, gentle rain began to fall. It was such an unusual rain shower that everybody everywhere went outside to see it.

At 12:10 p.m. precisely, the rain suddenly stopped and an enormous rainbow, longer and wider than anyone had ever seen before, spanned the heavens. But that wasn't all. Words began to appear on the rainbow in the same way messages flash across advertising signs in shop windows.

The first message read,

All Those Who Have Been Touched by This Rain
Will Have Their Sins Shown.

Sure enough, as people turned to look at each other, their faces began to change color...not just small spots, but large blocks of color: red, yellow, blue, purple and green. An assortment of colors appeared on every face.

A second message appeared on the rainbow just before it disappeared.

Jesus Is Coming Back in Seven Days
to Take All Those With Clean Faces.

The first thought on everyone's mind was to get clean. Inside the hour, the chemists' shops throughout the world were sold out of every kind of skin cleanser. But it did no good to rub the skin — in fact, it only intensified the colors.

Then someone remembered that the message had mentioned Jesus, and they knew enough to head for the nearest

---

[1]Retold with the author's permission. For the original story, see: Edward Hays, *The Ethiopian Tattoo Shop* (Leavenworth, KS: Forest of Peace Books, Inc., 1979).

shop selling Bibles. Others followed in droves, and there began the biggest Bible-reading marathon the world has even known. People everywhere were reading the Bible from cover to cover, looking for the answer to their deeply colored faces. Apart from a few rainbows here and there,[2] none with any writing on them, there seemed no answer in the Book.

Sunday came around, and the churches and cathedrals were packed to overflowing three hours before the services were due to start. Long lines formed outside as people strained to hear some words of explanation and hope. Sadly, most of the preachers called in sick that day, and those who did appear wore large paper bags over their heads. They had cut out slits for their eyes and mouths to enable them to see and speak, but still, none could give an explanation for the rainbow colors. The only preachers in the whole world that Sunday were the TV evangelists. People were greatly impresssed until someone pointed out that the programs were recorded a week in advance.

Then Monday morning came and even worse news broke. Someone, somewhere, somehow managed to crack the color code. He found out exactly which sin brought about which color — yellow for pride, green for jealousy, and so it went on. The news of the color code spread like wildfire around the world. All those who were burdened and outcast — the known sinners — could clearly see, on the faces of the doctors, teachers, lawyers and clergy, secret sins in abundance. For some, this was one of the lighter moments in a somewhat trying week.

Still, the problem of removing the color remained. Committees were formed in an attempt to find a solution. This was usually done over the phone so that those involved could keep their colored faces out of the public glare. But by Wednesday night, no one had found a way to clean the colored faces.

That night, a man and his wife sat down together. Sadly he looked at her green- yellow- and purple-stained face and tried to force a smile through orange lips.

[2]Gen. 9:13, Rev. 4:3, Rev. 10:1.

"Well," he said, "the seven days are up tomorrow, and neither of us are clean-faced. I want to tell you I'm really sorry for the way I've treated you. I never really listened when you spoke to me, and I was unfaithful to you a couple of times in the early years — not because I didn't love you, but — well, just because..."

His wife responded, "I'm sorry, too," she said. "I've been jealous of your success at the office and the way you get along so well with everyone. Sometimes it made me so angry. I'm sorry."

As they spoke, tears began to roll down their faces, and an amazing thing happened. Their faces began to change, the colors disappeared and a shining brightness replaced them.

The bad news about the color code had spread quickly around the world that Monday morning, but the good news, that if you were truly sorry for your sins and cried real tears of repentance, cleansing would come, spread even faster.

All over the world, people were admitting that they were sorry for their failures. And when they did, their faces became clean. And they were forgiven. And Jesus came back to take all those with clean faces.

Postscript

The way forward for each of us, whether clowns with white faces and baggy trousers or simply fools for Christ, raises similar challenges. What are we to do next? Where do we go for help?

There are no rules for holy fools. Jesus invites his followers on a journey, an adventure of faith.[1] This involves risking pain and giving up personal freedom. Remember:

Discipl<u>in</u>e
is
<u>in</u> Disciple

Enjoy the trip. Life is not a rehearsal.

It has been a great encouragement to me to read novels that contain the elements of holy folly. Here are just a couple that might be helpful:

1. *Christ Recrucified* by Nikos Kazantzakis[2] tells a modern version of the Passion. Manolios, the shepherd, is chosen to play the part of Jesus in the local Passion play. He seeks to fully understand his role — not just as an actor, but as one who would follow God. This has tragic and glorious results. The novel, the first by Kazantzakis, was written in a very short period.

2. *Brothers Karamosov* by the nineteenth-century Russian writer Feodor Dostoevski.[3] This is an extremely long book but well worth the effort. I would especially recommend the section about the life of the elder, Zossima.

[1]Matt. 11:25.

[2]Nikos Kazantzakis, *Christ Recrucified* (London: Faber and Faber, 1982), 332.

3Feodor Mikhailovich Dostoevski, *Brothers Karamosov* (London: Penguin Books, 1967), 332-79.

May the road rise to meet you,
the wind be always at your back
the sun shine brightly in your face
the rain fall soft upon your fields
and until we meet again
may the Lord hold you in the hollow of his hand.[4]

[4]Tradtional Celtic blessing.

The Clown's Prayer

"As I stumble through this life,
help me to create more laughter than tears,
dispense more happiness than gloom,
spread more cheer than despair.
Never let me become so indifferent
that I will fail to see the wonder
in the eyes of a child
or the twinkle in the eyes of the aged.
Never let me forget that my total effort
is to cheer people, make them happy
and forget at least momentarily
all the unpleasantness in their lives.
And in my final moment,
may I hear you whisper:
When you made my people smile,
you made me smile."

— Author Unknown

Bibliography

Bacci, L. *The Lift of St. Philip Neri*. Vol. 1. London: Kegan Paul & Co., 1902.

Bain, Roly. *Fools Rush In*. London: Marshall and Pickering, 1993.

Baker, Paul. *Of Minstrels, Monks, and Milkmen*. London: S.C.M., 1981.

Beck, Peggy. "In the Company of Laughter." *Parabola: The Magazine of Myth and Tradition III*. (Fall 1986): 58.

Bolton, Reg. *Circus in a Suitcase*. Bristol: Butterfingers Publishers, 1985.

Boys, C. V. *Soap Bubbles, Their Colors and Forces Which Mould Them*. New York: Dover Publications, Inc., 1959.

Britz, Heidi. *Children at Play: A Preparation for Life*. Edinburgh: Floris Books, 1972.

Brown, Margie. *A Clown Is Born*. San Francisco: self-published, 1982.

Budworth, G. *Much Ado About Knotting*. Horndean, England: International Guild of Knot Tyers, 1993.

Calvin, John. Book 1, chap. 11 and chap. 12 in *The Institutes of Christian Religion*. Translated by Henry Beveridge n.p.: James Clark & Co., Ltd., 1962.

Carlo. *The Juggling Book*. New York: Vintage Books, 1974.

Cassidy, J., and D. Stein. *The Unbelievable Bubble Book*. Palo Alto: Klutz Publications, 1987.

Central Board of Finance of the Church of England. *Alternative Service Book*, 1980.

Crowther, Carol. *Clowns and Clowning*. London: MacDonald, 1978.

Dean, Frank. *Will Rogers' Rope Tricks*. Colorado Springs: Western Horseman Publications, 1969.

De Bono, Edward. *Lateral Thinking: A Textbook of Creativity*. New York: Penguin Books, 1977.

De Paola, Tomie. *The Clown of God*. New York: Harcourt Brace Jovanovich, 1978.

Dostoevski, Feodor Mikhailovich. *Brothers Karamosov.* London: Penguin Books, 1967.

Endo, Sushaku. *Wonderful Fool.* Tokyo: Tuttle Publications, 1958.

Farley, Todd. *The Silent Prophet.* PA: Destiny Image Publishers, 1989.

Feit, Ken. interview by Michael Thoms, *Living and Free,* mid-seventies.

Finney, J. *Finding Faith Today: How Does It Happen?* Westlea, Swindon: Bible Society, 1992.

Forbes, Patrick. *The Gospel of Folly.* UK: Angel Press, 1988.

Fulghum, Robert. *All I Really Needed to Know I Learned in Kindergarten: Uncommon Thoughts on Common Things.* New York: Villard Books, 1988.

Furness-Jayne, Caroline. *String Figures and How to Make Them.* New York: Dover Publications, Inc., 1962.

Gardner, Martin. "The Soma Cube." chap. 6 in *More Mathematical Puzzles and Diversions.* New York: Penguin Books, 1962.

Gifford, D. "Iconographical Notes Towards a Definition of the Medieval Fool." *Journal of the Wadkig and Courtauld Institutes.* 37 (1974).

Harbin, Robert. *Secrets of Origami.* London: Oldbourne, 1963.

Paper Magic. London: Oldbourne, 1956.

Harper, M. *A New Way of Living.* London: Hodder and Stoughton, 1973.

Hays, Edward. *The Ethiopian Tattoo Shop.* Leavenworth, KS.: Forest of Peace Books, Inc., 1979.

Kazantzakis, Nikos. *Christ Recrucified.* London: Faber & Faber, 1982.

Lawrence, Brother. *The Practice of the Presence of God.* Mt. Vernon, NY: Peter Pauper Press, 1963.

Leitzman, W. *Visual Topology.* London: Chattoo & Windus, 1969.

Litherland, Janet. *The Clown Ministry Handbook.* Colorado Springs: Meriwether Publishing Ltd., 1982.

Everything New and Who's Who in Clown Ministry. Colorado Springs: Meriwether Publishing Ltd., 1993.

Makarios of Athos, Saint and Saint Makarios of Corinth, comps. *The Philokalia.* Venice, 1782.

Maurice, Edward. *Showmanship and Presentation.* Birmingham, England: Goodliffe Publications, 1946.

McClelland, J. C. *The Clown and the Crocodile.* Atlanta: John Knox Press, 1968.

O'Hara, Mary. *A Celebration of Love.* London: Hodder and Stoughton, 1985.

Paulat, Leo. *Jewish Tales: Eight Lights of the Hannukiya.* London: Beehive Books, 1986.

Petts, S. E. *Modern Parable.* Kent: Henry Walker Ltd., 1971.

Sadeh, Phinlas. "The Young Man and the Lawyer Who Was Princess." *Jewish Folk Tales.* London: Collins, 1990.

Saward, John. *Perfect Fools.* Oxford: Oxford University Press, 1978.

Shaffer, Floyd. *The Complete Floyd Shaffer Clown Ministry Workshop Kit.* Audiotapes of lectures given by Floyd Shaffer.

Sobel, Raoul, and David Francis. *Chaplin: Genesis of a Clown.* London: Quartet Books, 1979.

Solieri, Ferruvccio. *Commedia Dell'Arte Portraits.* Performed by Ferruvccio Solieri. Live, 1993.

Stolzenberg, Mark. *Clown of Circus and Stage.* New York: Sterling Publishing, 1978.

Twain, Mark. *The Adventures of Tom Sawyer.* New York: Grosset and Dunlop, Inc., 1946.

Van Der Post, L. *Yet Being Someone Other.* London: Hogarth Press, 1983.

Vanier, Jean. *Community and Growth.* London: D.L.T., 1979.

Wiley, Jack. *Basic Circus, Juggling, Unicycling, Bicycling and Clowning Skills.* n.p.: Solipaz Publishing Co., 1983.

Wilson, John. *One of the Richest Gifts.* Edinburgh: Hansel Press, 1981.

ABOUT THE AUTHOR

Philip Noble, a.k.a. "Rainbow," is an Episcopalian minister and evangelist from Scotland who has been involved in the visual arts for many years as a clown, storyteller and workshop leader. Originally trained in pure science and theology, he has developed play and performance skills that are suitable for audiences of all ages, using paper, string and a selection of simple objects.

Philip has conducted workshops and given performances throughout the United Kingdom for over fifteen years. He has also traveled widely in his role as evangelist-storyteller-clown, visiting the United States, Holland, Sweden, Switzerland, France, Portugal, Zambia, South Africa and Japan. He has performed in a variety of settings, from schools, churches and libraries, to theaters, prisons and outdoor festivals. He spent three years in Papua, New Guinea in the early 1970s. There, he learned how to make a large variety of string figures from the local people.

He has written books on string figures and has contributed to several other books on origami, string figures and clown ministry, including *The Clown Ministry Handbook* and *Everything New and Who's Who in Clown Ministry.*

Though Philip continues to give formal performances, he really sees himself as an "itinerant gladness scatterer," constantly ready to share the wonder of God's creativity. His goals are twofold: to awaken the sense of wonder in simple things through his performances, and to encourage all to playfully develop their creative gifts to the glory of God through his workshops.

ORDER FORM

MERIWETHER PUBLISHING LTD.
P.O. BOX 7710
COLORADO SPRINGS, CO 80933
TELEPHONE: (719) 594-4422

Please send me the following books:

_____ **Fool of the Kingdom #CC-B202**   **$12.95**
by Philip D. Noble
How to be an effective clown minister

_____ **The Clown Ministry Handbook #CC-B163**   **$10.95**
by Janet Litherland
The first and most complete text on the art of clown ministry

_____ **Everything New and Who's Who in**   **$10.95**
Clown Ministry #CC-B126
by Janet Litherland
Profiles of clown ministers plus 75 skits for special days

_____ **Clown Skits for Everyone #CC-B147**   **$12.95**
by Happy Jack Feder
A delightful guide to becoming a performing clown

_____ **Clown Act Omnibus #CC-B118**   **$12.95**
by Wes McVicar
Everything you need to know about clowning

_____ **You Can Do Christian Puppets #CC-B196**   **$10.95**
by Bea Carlton
A basic guide to Christian puppetry

_____ **Teaching With Bible Games #CC-B108**   **$10.95**
by Ed Dunlop
20 "kid-tested" contests for Christian education

**These and other fine Meriwether Publishing books are available at
your local bookstore or direct from the publisher. Use the handy
order form on this page.**

NAME: _____

ORGANIZATION NAME: _____

ADDRESS: _____

CITY:_____ STATE: _____ ZIP: _____

PHONE: _____
   ❏ **Check Enclosed**
   ❏ **Visa or MasterCard #** _____
                               Expiration
Signature: _____ *Date:* _____
        (required for Visa/MasterCard orders)

COLORADO RESIDENTS: Please add 3% sales tax.
SHIPPING: Include $2.75 for the first book and 50¢ for each additional book ordered.

   ❏ *Please send me a copy of your complete catalog of books and plays.*

ORDER FORM

MERIWETHER PUBLISHING LTD.
P.O. BOX 7710
COLORADO SPRINGS, CO 80933
TELEPHONE: (719) 594-4422

Please send me the following books:

_____ **Fool of the Kingdom #CC-B202**   **$12.95**
by Philip D. Noble
How to be an effective clown minister

_____ **The Clown Ministry Handbook #CC-B163**   **$10.95**
by Janet Litherland
The first and most complete text on the art of clown ministry

_____ **Everything New and Who's Who in**   **$10.95**
Clown Ministry #CC-B126
by Janet Litherland
Profiles of clown ministers plus 75 skits for special days

_____ **Clown Skits for Everyone #CC-B147**   **$12.95**
by Happy Jack Feder
A delightful guide to becoming a performing clown

_____ **Clown Act Omnibus #CC-B118**   **$12.95**
by Wes McVicar
Everything you need to know about clowning

_____ **You Can Do Christian Puppets #CC-B196**   **$10.95**
by Bea Carlton
A basic guide to Christian puppetry

_____ **Teaching With Bible Games #CC-B108**   **$10.95**
by Ed Dunlop
20 "kid-tested" contests for Christian education

**These and other fine Meriwether Publishing books are available at
your local bookstore or direct from the publisher. Use the handy
order form on this page.**

NAME: _____

ORGANIZATION NAME: _____

ADDRESS: _____

CITY:_____ STATE: _____ ZIP: _____

PHONE: _____
   ❑ **Check Enclosed**
   ❑ **Visa or MasterCard #** _____

Signature: _____ *Expiration
Date:* _____

(required for Visa/MasterCard orders)

COLORADO RESIDENTS: Please add 3% sales tax.
SHIPPING: Include $2.75 for the first book and 50¢ for each additional book ordered.

   ❑ *Please send me a copy of your complete catalog of books and plays.*